HAUNTED [
OF THE CAROLINAS

Cheralyn Lambeth

4880 Lower Valley Road, Atglen, Pennsylvania 19310

Cover Image Theater Chairs © James Steidl. *Photo Courtesy Bigstockphotos.com.*
All photos unless otherwise noted are copyrighted by the author.
Back Cover Photo: The interior of Dana Auditorium, Guilford College, Greensboro
North Carolina.

Schiffer Books are available at special discounts for bulk purchases for sales promotions
or premiums. Special editions, including personalized covers, corporate imprints, and
excerpts can be created in large quantities for special needs. For more information contact
the publisher:

Schiffer Publishing Ltd.
4880 Lower Valley Road
Atglen, PA 19310
Phone: (610) 593-1777; Fax: (610) 593-2002
E-mail: Info@schifferbooks.com

For the largest selection of fine reference books on this and related subjects, please visit
our web site at **www.schifferbooks.com**
We are always looking for people to write books on new and related subjects. If you have
an idea for a book please contact us at the above address.

This book may be purchased from the publisher. Include $5.00 for shipping. Please try
your bookstore first. You may write for a free catalog.

In Europe, Schiffer books are distributed by
Bushwood Books
6 Marksbury Ave.
Kew Gardens
Surrey TW9 4JF England
Phone: 44 (0) 20 8392-8585; Fax: 44 (0) 20 8392-9876
E-mail: info@bushwoodbooks.co.uk
Website: www.bushwoodbooks.co.uk

Designed by Stephanie Daugherty
Type set in Rosemary Roman/New Baskerville BT

ISBN: 978-0-7643-3327-9
Printed in The United States of America

DEDICATION

To my parents, Jay and Phyllis, with great love and thanks for not only letting me pursue the performing arts, but encouraging me to succeed; and to my sister, Michelle, in fond memory of our own ghost "Fleeting Feather."

ACKNOWLEDGMENTS

As my first book, this project has given me a great deal of appreciation for just how much time and energy goes into such a work, and I couldn't have done it without the help of numerous people and institutions. In addition to sincerely thanking all the people mentioned by name in the book for granting me their time and knowledge in countless interviews, I also would like to thank the following:

Drew Allison and Vania Reckard at Grey Seal Puppets for their continuing advice, support, and patience in giving me the time off needed to complete this work; Samantha Burroughs and Meredith Rapkin for putting me on the trail of stories I didn't even realize were out there; my uncle Fred Saverance, whose own research into South Carolina history came in handy on more than one occasion; Herb Garmen for his incredible inside knowledge of the theater buildings at the University of North Carolina-Chapel Hill (and for his willingness to share it!); Michael Coker and the other curators at The South Carolina Historical Society in Charleston for cheerfully answering silly questions and hunting up all sorts of seemingly unrelated data, and for finding information I needed before I even knew I needed it; the staff at Davis and Wilson Libraries at the University of North Carolina-Chapel Hill for unerringly pointing me in the right direction; the staff at the East Boulevard (Charlotte) FedEx/Kinko's for their helpfulness above and beyond the call of duty as I struggled to prepare my first manuscript for mailing; my friend and fellow author Pamela Kinney, who encouraged me to follow through with the idea of a haunted theaters book, and who introduced me to the great folks at Schiffer; and finally my editor, Dinah Roseberry, whose understanding with and patience for a first-time author knows no limit. Without all of these kind and supportive people, this book would never have been.

CONTENTS

INTRODUCTION

> **HORATIO:** *O day and night, but this is wondrous strange!*
>
> **HAMLET:** *And therefore as a stranger give it welcome. There are more things in heaven and earth, Horatio, Than are dreamt of in your philosophy.*
>
> ~*Hamlet, Act I scene 5*

As a theatre and film professional, I've had the opportunity to work in and visit a wide variety of beautiful and historic theatrical houses. More often than not, each theater has its own story (or even multiple stories) of ghosts and hauntings, particularly if the building is an old one, and I've thoroughly enjoyed listening to and collecting them (and sometimes even experiencing them!) over the years. I have always been interested in theater ghosts and ghost stories, not only from a professional standpoint, but from a personal interest in history as well. When you see a ghost or other haunting, you have a rare opportunity to get an actual glimpse at a piece of the past.

It's very true that theaters are notorious for being haunted. The amount of energy that goes into a theatrical production is vast, from the actors pouring themselves into their roles, to the crew rushing around in frantic haste performing their jobs, even to the emotional involvement of the

audience. After weeks, months, even years of this repetitive activity, all that spent energy can get trapped in the fabric of a building, presenting ideal conditions for a "residual haunting"—what paranormal researchers believe is a replayed haunting in which there is no intelligent entity involved, just a "playback" of past sights, sounds, and even smells, an echo of past events. It is theorized that these types of hauntings are the result of personal energy making an imprint on the surrounding environment and later playing back like a video tape; and there is no doubt that a great deal of personal energy and intense emotion goes into the production of a play. Also in that vein, the constant repetition of actions (which is also certainly true of the same play being performed night after night) could wear a "groove" in the surrounding environment as well; if that theory is true, it is easy to see how something like that might well replay itself again and again. The vast amount of energy present in a theater building could also easily give an "intelligent haunting"—one where there *is* an intelligent entity involved—the energy it needs to manifest itself.

At least, so the theory goes. Skeptics might claim that an exhausted actor or crew member, in a dark, half-empty mysterious theater, are simply prone to misinterpreting the common creaks and other strange noises that any old building would make over time.

Break a Leg!

Theatre people are indeed a very superstitious lot. So much can go wrong in the production of a play—a forgotten line, a costume that gets torn right before it goes on stage, movable set or prop pieces that don't work when they should—that theater personnel can't be blamed for doing whatever they can to ensure a good production. Many actors and crew members have their own individual rituals they observe (such as carrying a lucky talisman) in addition to the more well-known superstitions observed in theatrical houses the world over. The saying "break a leg," for example, comes from an old term for bending one's knees. If a performer's knees are locked, and they are (understandably!) nervous, they can very easily faint. This reminder to relax the knees, and just to relax in general, has taken the place of telling someone "good luck," and has even moved out of the theatrical realm into common usage.

Whistle While You Work

Another interesting theatrical superstition, that it's considered unlucky to whistle on or off stage, actually has its basis in historical fact. Theatrical rigging—the series of ropes and pulleys that in the old days of theatre raised and lowered the sets and later lighting—has its origins in the rigging used to raise and lower the sails on ships. Stage crews were at one time made up of off-duty sailors hired off of ships in port. Since sailors, and by extension theatrical riggers, depended on coded whistles to communicate sail or scene changes, actors who whistled could confuse them into changing set pieces out of order. (Or you could also just as easily get a sandbag dropped on your head by mistake!)

A Failing Curse

And then of course there's "the Scottish play"—it is considered *extremely* unlucky to perform, quote lines from, or even say the name of Shakespeare's *Macbeth* in a theater for fear of bringing about the curse that's said to be associated with this work. Several theories attempt to explain this "curse," one of them being that the descendants of Macbeth alive during Shakespeare's time were angry with the playwright for casting the poor guy in such a bad light, and so cursed the play. Another theory is that the witches' chants in the play were supposedly taken from actual incantations used to summon demons, and if uttered, will conjure all sorts of evil spirits and bad luck. (Many actors are reluctant to quote these lines even in a production.)

Historically, producing *Macbeth* was often the last-ditch effort of a failing theatre—if your company was about to close due to lack of business, you put on *Macbeth* in the hopes of drawing crowds—and so the play really did become the curse of failing theatres.

Whatever the origins for the curse surrounding "the Scottish play," it's certainly true that many production companies that have attempted to perform this tragedy have many times met with tragedy themselves. During the very first production of *Macbeth* in 1606, the boy actor playing Lady Macbeth died mysteriously backstage during the performance; the play has been dogged by bad luck ever since.

Ghostly Characters

Along with superstition, ghosts play an integral part in the world of theatre, both on and off the stage. Many plays contain ghostly characters—four of Shakespeare's tragedies involve ghosts, not only the aforementioned *Macbeth*, but also *Hamlet, Julius Caesar,* and *Richard III* (which has a grand total of eleven ghosts appearing throughout the play!). So it is interesting to note that several mainstream theatrical traditions actually do have their basis in ghost stories.

As a general rule, theaters are closed (or "dark") one day a week, usually Mondays. According to theatrical lore, this is supposedly to give the ghosts there a chance to perform their own plays (although in reality it conveniently gives actors and crew a day off to rest from a busy weekend!). The "ghost light" that is left burning on the lower right hand stage of an empty theater is set there for several reasons—either to ward off ghosts, or to give them enough light to see by (and thereby keep them from getting angry and pulling malicious pranks!), or—more logically—to keep theater personnel from falling in the dark and getting killed, to possibly become ghosts themselves.

Finally, a well-known term for a theatrical performer, *thespian,* is derived from the Greek actor Thespis. He is credited with being the first performer in the history of theater to speak individual lines on stage on what is believed to be November 23, 534 BC. It is said that his ghost even now is responsible for any unexplainable problems or mischief that might hit a production, especially if it

falls on November 23. Quite often, many theaters will avoid holding a production on that date if they can possibly manage it!

With all the superstitions and rituals surrounding the theatrical world, along with the historical and often mysterious aspects of the production houses themselves, it's little wonder that many theaters around the globe have their share of ghost stories. And regardless of whether or not one is truly a believer, much of the day-to-day operation of a theater company is strongly influenced by their ghosts—so in that sense, it is very real indeed.

Following are just a few of the myths and legends surrounding theater houses in North and South Carolina, an area not only rich in history and famous ghosts (such as the infamous pirate Blackbeard), but in theatrical tradition—and theatrical ghosts—as well. I hope you'll enjoy reading about these lesser-known Carolina ghosts as we start on our tour of *Haunted Theaters of the Carolinas*.

GLOSSARY OF THEATRE AND ARCHITECTURAL TERMS

Apron

A part of the stage projecting into the audience; the stage area in front of the proscenium arch.

Arena

A theatre in which the audience sits on all sides of the performance area.

Auditorium

The part of the theater where the audience is accommodated; the House. Auditorium can also describe the entire theater building.

Backstage

Any part of the stage not in the acting area during a performance.

Beaux-Arts

An architectural style combining elements of Greek/Roman architecture with Renaissance ideas. A favored style for grand public buildings (such as theaters), the term originated in the École des Beaux Arts architectural school in Paris, and often features columns, balconies, lavish decorations, and grand staircases.

"Black Box"

A simple, plain performance space, usually a large square room with black walls and a flat floor.

"Boards"

A slang term for the stage area.

Box Seats/Seating

A private seat or row of seats in a box at the theater where an individual or group can watch the performance set apart from the general audience.

Catwalk

A narrow, elevated walkway above the stage.

Curtain

The drapery which conceals the stage from the audience. This term can also be used to describe the action of the House Curtain coming down at the end of an act or the play, as well as the last piece of action on the stage before the House Curtain comes down.

Dark/Dark House

A theater which is closed or inactive, either temporarily or permanently; Mondays are usually "dark" days after a weekend of performances.

Deck

The stage floor area.

Dimmer switch

Electrical device which controls the intensity of the light in the lighting instruments for both the house and stage. Dimmers are normally numbered in sequence, and controlled by the electrics technician from the light board.

Downstage
The front of the stage, towards the audience.

Electrics
A general term used to describe both the lighting equipment in the theater and the members of the lighting crew. Also referred to as "LX."

Front of House
Refers to audience/production services such as parking, concessions, program distributing, and ushering.

Fly/Fly Space
The space above the stage in which scenery, lighting equipment, etc. are hung invisible to the audience, and from which they are raised and lowered ("flown in/out") during the course of the performance.

Gallery, Gods
The highest section of the theater; a section at the back or sides without seats where people can stand to watch a performance, usually raised.

Ghost Light
A light left on the stage overnight and/or when the stage is not in use for safety. The ghost light is traditionally left burning on the down stage right area.

Green Room

A room close to the stage for the actors to gather in, to relax and prepare for their performance The term is believed to come from medieval times when dramatic performances were given on the village green; a tent would be set up there for the actors to change costumes in, hence "Green Room." The color green is also soothing, and helps the performers to relax before and after they go on stage.

Grid

The arrangement of metal and wooden slats above the stage where the fly system and/or scenery and lighting equipment are mounted.

"Hemp House"

A theater where the lighting/scenery is flown in and out manually on a rope (hemp) and pulley system; in the old days of theater, this was often done by off-duty sailors in port. Nowadays most fly systems are flown electrically by computer.

House

The theater building; also the people in the theater, the audience.

House Right

The right-hand side of the seating area as the audience faces the stage; stage left.

House Left

The left-hand side of the seating area as the audience faces the stage; stage right.

Legs

Vertical strips of fabric, usually black, used mainly for masking the sides of the stage.

Load In

The term used to describe the installation of a show's scenery, electrics, and other elements into the theater space. The opposite is Load Out.

Masking

Drapery or flats used to frame the stage, and stop the audience from seeing the backstage areas.

Mezzanine/Balcony

The lowest balcony in the theater.

Offstage

Out of sight of the audience.

Onstage

In sight of the audience, on the stage itself.

(The) Orchestra, The Stalls

Seats on the lower part of the theater (orchestra seating).

Orchestra pit

The area where the musicians play, usually directly in front of the stage, often sunken below the seating sections.

Playhouse

A common Elizabethan-era term for a theater, still used by many theater houses today.

Prop, Property

Any object held or used on stage by an actor for use in furthering the plot. Smaller props are referred to as "hand props," while larger props may also be set decoration, such as a chair or table. If the item is not touched by a performer for any reason, it is considered simply a set decoration, part of the scenery. If it is touched or used by the actor during the course of the performance, it is a prop.

Proscenium, Proscenium arch

The archway over the stage which separates the stage and the auditorium.

Rake/raked stage

A stage floor or seating area built at an incline, usually with the rear side being higher.

Site Specific

A play which is created or specifically modified to use the character of the performance space to the greatest advantage. Site specific spaces are usually locations which are not normally used for showcasing theatre, but have another primary function (warehouse, mansion, abandoned military bunker, etc.).

Sound/lighting/tech booth

A small room at the back of the theater (often above the last tier of seating) that houses the sound, lighting, and/ or special effects boards controlling the technical aspects of the production, along with the tech crew members who operate them.

Stage
The part of the theater on which the actor performs.

Stage left
The side of the stage on the left when facing the audience; house right.

Stage Manager
The crew member responsible for the smooth running of a performance. Before a production opens, the Stage Manager attends rehearsals and meetings with other members of the production, and is often responsible for coordinating all the various aspects of the production in a smaller theatre company. During the performance, the Stage Manager will cue the actors as well as the sound, light, and scenic changes, although many times this function will also be performed by an Assistant Stage Manager (ASM).

Stage right
The side of the stage on the right when facing the audience; house left.

Tabs
Curtains separating the stage from the audience.

Tech or Techie
A general slang term for any member of the technical crew of a production.

Tech or Technical rehearsal
A rehearsal primarily for the purpose of practicing the technical elements of a play, such as lights and sound.

Theater
A building where acting takes place, including a movie house/cinema.

Theatre
The world of this type of acting, or the world of acting in general; the art itself. The term comes from the ancient Greek work *theatron,* which means "place of seeing."

Theatre in the round
Any theater where the audience is seated on every side of the stage.

Thrust
A stage that extends out into the audience, so that the audience is seated on three sides of it.

Upstage
The back half of the stage furthest from the audience. This term came from the raked stage, where the back area is "up" from the forward ("downstage") area.

Vaudeville
Stage variety shows generally composed of short acts such as song-and-dance routines, comedy performances, and juggling. The term is believed to have come from the French vaudevire (light popular song), which is possibly short for chanson du Vau de Vire (song of Vau de Vire, a valley in northwest France), or for vauder (to go) plus virer (to see). Vaudeville touring shows were very popular in America before the introduction of motion pictures with sound ("talkies") in the mid 1900s. Wardrobe costumes, or the people responsible for them.

Wardrobe

Costumes, or the people responsible for them. The wardrobe master/mistress is the crew member in charge of the costuming.

Wings

The "backstage" or parts of a stage off to the left and right, not seen by the audience.

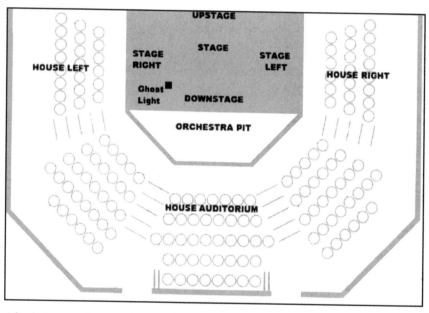

A basic layout of a thrust/proscenium theater, showing the names and locations of theater space elements. *Illustration by the author.*

NORTH CAROLINA

WATERSIDE THEATRE

THE LOST COLONY
OUTDOOR DRAMA

ROANOKE ISLAND

> One of North Carolina's greatest mysteries, the people of this first British settlement in North America seemed to vanish without a trace. Do their ghosts haunt the theater that stands on the site of their former home?

Of all haunted locations in the Carolinas (both theatrical and otherwise), perhaps one of the best known is the Lost Colony, part of the Fort Raleigh National Historic site. Located on the island of Manteo, just between the North Carolina mainland and the Outer Banks barrier islands, the Lost Colony is the location of the first British settlement established in the New World. Its inhabitants met a mysterious fate which has been a source of fascination for historians to this day. The outdoor drama chronicling the tale is the oldest in North America, with the theater complex situated near the actual site of the original colony.

The Outer Banks region of North Carolina is an area that is unusual both historically and geographically. Many paranormal researchers speculate that geography can play a large part in determining if an area is prone to

The Waterside Theatre as it appeared in 1987. *Photo courtesy of the author.*

"haunting" activity, and there is no doubt that the Outer Banks are geographically unique. There have been theories that large deposits of limestone, quartz, and/or water have some effect on residual hauntings, as each of these can hold electromagnetic charges; and certainly all three of these are abundant in this area. The unusual arrangement of the barrier islands, along with dangerously shallow water and unpredictable weather, make the Carolina coastline a difficult stretch of ocean for ships to navigate, and over 2,000 shipwrecks to date have been claimed in this area that has come to be known as "The Graveyard of the Atlantic."

Historically, local folk tales claim the Devil himself was a frequent visitor to these parts, giving rise to such place names as Kill Devil Hills in nearby Nag's Head, North Carolina. Various tribes of Native Americans lived in the area, and much of the land was sacred to them both as living/hunting territories and as burial grounds. The infamous Blackbeard the pirate preyed on unsuspecting ships in these waters, and met his end on Ocracoke Island in 1718; his ghost is said to stalk the Outer Banks as well. And finally—depending on which source you reference—this spot is said to mark one of the points of the Bermuda (or Devil's) Triangle, another section of the Atlantic Ocean supposedly home to mysterious paranormal activity and unexplained disappearances.

All in all, a very formidable set of circumstances. Little wonder the area would be prone to being haunted!

The historical facts of the colony's founding are fairly well documented. The idea for establishing a permanent settlement in the New World had long been building in the mind of naval explorer Sir Walter Raleigh, and in 1585 he mounted an expedition to search for a suitable place for such an endeavor. The expedition came upon what seemed a likely spot on Roanoke Island, and approximately 100 men set about the task of building a settlement there. For a while, things went well, but dwindling supplies and growing hostilities with the local native tribes forced the settlers to abandon their attempt, and to return to England with Sir Frances Drake less than one year later.

Sir Walter would not allow himself to be discouraged, however, and the following year he tried again. In 1587, Queen Elizabeth I granted him permission to send another expedition to America; and shortly thereafter, a group of 117 men, women, and children under the leadership of Governor John White set sail from Plymouth, England. Their original destination was Chesapeake Bay, Virginia, where each settler had been promised their own tract of land. However, once the ship landed at Roanoke Island, the ship's captain refused to sail any further north for fear of uncertain weather. He left the colonists there to fend for themselves, promising to return at a later date with more supplies.

Under Governor White's leadership, the settlers slowly managed to restore and add to the original settlement, and the colony began to grow. The Governor befriended Manteo, chief of the Croatoan tribe, and Manteo's people were of great help to the colonists as they struggled to build a home for themselves. Manteo and Governor White also worked together in an attempt to make peace between the settlers and the other native tribes who had been less than happy to share their land with the Europeans, but their attempts were largely unsuccessful. Several skirmishes erupted between the colonists and the natives, and tensions between the groups continued to grow.

Meanwhile, the colonists continued to try and establish some structure of their normal lives in this strange new land; and on August 18, 1587, the first European child was born in the New World. Granddaughter of Governor White, the baby was christened Virginia Dare, and her birth was looked on as a momentous occasion; both by the colonists, who saw her as a sign of new hope for their struggling colony, and by Manteo's people, who were fascinated by her pale skin and blue eyes.

In spite of the hope and excitement brought about by Virginia's birth, the colony continued in a desperate struggle for survival. Food and other needed supplies were running dangerously low, and Governor White was forced to return to England for provisions. Upon his arrival, however, his ship was conscripted into military service for the war with Spain, and he was unable to return to America. The governor even petitioned Queen Elizabeth for permission to take the much-needed supplies to the colony, but it was almost three years later before he was able to find passage back to Roanoke.

What happened next has long been a source of speculation for historians and mystery-lovers alike. When Governor White arrived at the island, the colonists—every man, woman, and child—had seemingly vanished into thin air. No sign of them could be seen except for a rusting suit of armor on the beach, and the letters "CRO" carved into a nearby tree; "CROATOAN" was also carved into one of the palisades at the settlement itself. Governor White, and later Sir Walter Raleigh, searched for the missing colonists, but never found any other trace of them.

After the disappearance of the colony, it was largely forgotten. As more and more explorers came to the New World to establish their own settlements, discovering the fate of the colonists became less and less of a priority. A few attempts were made by other settlers to find the missing colonists; when John Smith and the Jamestown colonists arrived in Virginia in 1607, Smith took up the search, but like Governor White and Sir Walter Raleigh before him, could find no solid proof of where they may have gone.

In the following years, evidence of the colonists' fate was slow to emerge. Occasionally, unusual artifacts or previously-unknown documents would be discovered that hinted at what may have become of the colonists, but for the most part, no genuine clues had ever been found. As the colony's 300th anniversary approached in the 1880s, new theories presented by both the media and the academic community prompted a renewed interest in the story. Some of the theories which are debated even today are that the colonists may have simply left the depleted settlement in search of food elsewhere; many historians believe that the words "CROATOAN" and the letters "CRO" found carved at the colony site indicate they had moved on to the nearby Croatoan Island. Others believe the colonists may have perished in an attack by one of the unfriendly native tribes, or even the Spanish who were also attempting to establish themselves in the New World at that time; while there is no other sign of warfare other than the rusting suit of armor on the beach, the fact that the colonists' homes had been pulled down and a military-style fortification constructed in their place seems to lend some weight to this theory. Still others speculate that the carved letters indicate the colonists were taken in by Manteo's people, the friendly Croatoan. It is interesting to note that the present-day Lumbee, an Eastern Carolina tribe who are the descendants of the Croatoan, have blond hair and blue eyes, a possible indication of European ancestry.

In 1937—the 350th anniversary of the colony's founding—a series of mysterious rocks unearthed in eastern North Carolina seemed to solve the mystery at last. The first of these stones was found in a swamp sixty miles west of Roanoke Island, and was covered with strange carvings that, after study, seemed to be a message from Eleanor Dare. The markings appeared to indicate that the colonists had fled from Roanoke Island after falling under attack from one of the unfriendly native tribes. Almost forty other similar stones were found throughout the Southeast over the next three years, and when put together, seemed to relate an incredible tale of the colonists' travels as far south as Georgia. The media took up the tale with relish, and scoffed at the academic world's skepticism of the supposed artifacts; in the end, however, it was the academic world who had the last laugh when an investigative reporter exposed the entire story as an elaborate hoax in 1940. True or not, each new theory and discovery concerning the ill-fated settlement inspired a continuing curiosity about its fate, and a desire to celebrate its contribution to our nation's history. By the early 1900s, the residents of Roanoke Island had begun to work on a special project commemorating the 350th anniversary in 1937 of the birth of Virginia Dare.

North Carolina resident and Pulitzer-Prize winning playwright Paul Green was commissioned to adapt the story into a play. Green's work was designed to be performed outdoors on Roanoke Island itself, and his outdoor drama—the first of its kind in North America— was set on a massive scale and filled with symphonic music, drama, and dance. He also intended it to be the "people's theater"—theatre in which plays are produced by and for the people, for their enjoyment and not just for monetary gain. Meanwhile, the citizens of Roanoke Island set about building the outdoor stage as a project of President Franklin Roosevelt's Works Progress Administration. The employment provided by the theater's construction and the uplifting nature of Green's play both combined to lift people's spirits during the Great Depression, and on July 4, 1937, *The Lost Colony* opened to a packed house despite the current economic hardship.

Originally, the show was intended to run only through the end of that summer. However, as audiences continued to pour in throughout the season with favorable reviews, speculation began as to whether or not the production could become permanent; and when President Roosevelt himself attended in August, the show's future seasons were assured.

Since then, the production has run for more than seventy summers almost without interruption, in spite of numerous challenges and outright disasters. The show was briefly suspended during World War II for four years as the threat of German U-boats prowling the North Carolina coast made a blackout necessary. In 1947, the Waterside Theatre was lost in a fire that destroyed it completely, but it was quickly rebuilt by local residents. And in 1960, the building was once again lost to the elements as Hurricane Donna hit the island and swept much of the theater into the adjoining Pamlico Sound; but once again, it was reconstructed just in time for the 1961 season. Millions of people have packed the Waterside Theatre each summer ever since to see the beloved outdoor drama.

It was here, as a member of the drama's costuming crew, that I had one of my own most unsettling paranormal experiences. During the summer of 1987, The Lost Colony was celebrating the 50th anniversary of the outdoor drama's debut, in addition to the 400th anniversary of the colony's founding, and the energy in the atmosphere was high. Many of my fellow crew and cast members talked of having seen apparitions or heard disembodied voices and other unusual sounds throughout the course of the summer—as the costume shop supervisor only half-jokingly commented, there was "much spiritual unrest" that year.

One of the dancers confided in me that he had been napping on the sofa in his apartment at Morrison Grove (the nearby housing complex that is provided for the Lost Colony staff) when he woke suddenly to see two people in period dress standing at the foot of the sofa. He stared at them for several moments, until he blinked and looked away; when he looked back, they had vanished. Another cast member stated that he had been sitting in his living room late one night, and was startled to hear a disembodied voice suddenly whisper, "Don't be scared,"

A performance of *The Lost Colony*. *Photo courtesy of the author.*

into his ear. Good advice, perhaps, but probably not easy to follow at that point!

My own experience took place as I was finishing up work after a performance late one night. The audience and most of the other crew and cast had gone for the evening, and there were only a handful of us left in the theater. I was standing in the hallway of the stage left building, sorting costume laundry, when I heard footsteps coming up behind me on the wooden floor. Thinking it was another of the crew, I pulled my work aside to let them pass. As the footsteps came up beside me, I glanced over to see who was walking by, and was shocked to find that there was no one there. The footsteps continued down the hall to the door at the far end, at which point the door opened and closed by itself. I well remember standing frozen in place, staring at the door for several seconds, before I turned and quickly scooted into the costume shop where I knew there were other people, and told them my tale. None of the other costume staff seemed really surprised to hear my story, or surprised that I didn't want to be left alone anywhere in the theater the rest of that night!

The Lost Colony has continued to enchant audiences ever since, carrying on its tradition of almost-uninterrupted productions in spite of further tragedy. In September of 2007, a fire ripped through the theater and surrounding support buildings, destroying the costume shop and nearly seventy years of costumes and other artifacts and memorabilia. Fortunately, the seating amphitheater and the sets were saved, as were many of the costumes that were either at the dry cleaners or on display in the North Carolina Museum of History in Raleigh. But once again, the citizens of Roanoke as well as members from the film and theater industries donated money, supplies, time, and labor to make certain new costumes would be ready in time for the 2008 season. The National Park Service made rebuilding the costume shop and other damaged areas of the theater a priority, and just as in years past, everything was completed in the nick of time and the show opened right on schedule.

Today, Roanoke Island and *The Lost Colony* (both the Fort Raleigh site and the play itself) are regularly visited by archaeologists, historians, and those who are curious to learn more about the story of the ill-fated settlement. Solid archaeological clues as to the whereabouts of the colonists still have yet to be discovered, and their fate is as much a mystery today as it was 400 years ago. But their story is not forgotten, and perhaps their ghosts even now are witness to Paul Green's dream of "people's theater" that becomes a reality with every performance.

MCGINNIS THEATRE/ MESSICK THEATRE ARTS CENTER

EAST CAROLINA UNIVERSITY, GREENVILLE

> A historic building on this university campus that was once a teacher training school now serves as the home of its School of Theatre and Dance—and quite possibly the home of former staff and students.

As part of the University of North Carolina system, East Carolina University (ECU) is one of the fastest growing campuses in the state. Founded in 1907 as East Carolina Teacher's Training School, the institution (as its name implies) was originally established to train academic instructors for North Carolina, especially the eastern part of the state. As the school continued to grow, its curriculum expanded, and its name changed to East Carolina Teacher's College, then to East Carolina College, and finally to East Carolina University in 1967 when it joined the UNC system. Today, the university offers degree programs in over 100 areas of study, with historical strengths in education, medicine, and theater. The School of Theatre and Dance features productions by both the East Carolina Playhouse (student theatre) and the East Carolina Summer Theatre, a professional company.

Although the College of Fine Arts and Communication (which includes the School of Theatre and Dance) was not officially created at ECU until 2003, its roots date back to the beginning of the school's history. One of the early buildings on the campus was the four-room Model School, constructed in 1914 as a practice school for teachers in training. Students at the college could walk to the school through the wooded western portion of campus, and develop their teaching skills by working with the youngsters of the Greenville city school system. A second story was added to the building in 1917. Eventually, however, the growing enrollment at the college quickly outgrew the practice school, and the building was razed in 1927 to make way for a more modern facility.

In 1928, the "New Model School" opened on the site of the site of the former building, and served both the college as a teacher training facility and the city of Greenville as an elementary school. Student enrollment and staff continued to grow over the next forty-four years, and during the 1953-54 school year, East Carolina College renamed the building the Wahl-Coates Laboratory School in honor of Miss Dora Coates and Miss Frances Wahl, two former teachers and supervisors of the school during its formative years.

As the College continued to increase in student enrollment and programs, a need for yet another facility became evident. In the latter part of the 1960s, planning was initiated for a new Wahl-Coates elementary school. ECU collaborated with the city in 1972 to open Wahl-Coates Public School at a site off-campus, relieving ECU of actually providing elementary classroom space. The university retained the building, and plans got underway to remodel it for other uses.

Over the years, the building has undergone several renovations and additions as well as name changes. In 1951, an auditorium space had been built adjacent to the Wahl-Coates School, and was meant to serve as the school auditorium and college theater. Today, both the former school and the now attached auditorium are being used as the Messick Theatre Arts Center, named for former ECU president John Decatur Messick, who served the University from 1947 to 1959. The arts complex serves the School of Theatre and Dance, with classrooms and studios in the former Wahl-Coates School building. The attached McGinnis Auditorium has a costume shop in the basement, storage space, and, of course, ghosts.

Named in honor of another ECU president, Howard Justus McGinnis, McGinnis Auditorium has its share of campus ghost stories. One school legend tells of how a young drama student in the 1960s was supposed to play the lead in a musical, but was killed in an automobile accident before the production went up. About twenty years later in the 1980s, that same play was scheduled to run again. Another student was alone in the theater late one night practicing and recording piano music for the production when a folding chair on the stage collapsed for no apparent reason. Frightened, the student quickly left the building. When later she replayed the tape of her music, she could hear a female voice singing the lyrics to the song, even though she had been alone at the time.

Is McGinnis's ghost that of the young student killed in a car accident? This is not the only story of a ghostly female voice captured on tape. Another account tells of how a recording was made on stage of a woman playing the piano and a man singing. When the tape was played back, a woman's voice was heard singing along. Still other versions say that only the woman's voice was heard.

Many members of the university community, mostly students, believe the female ghost may actually be that of Dr. Lucille Charles, who was a professor in the drama department from 1946 until her death in March 1965. Reports have been made of a figure in white who floats across the stage, as well as unusual noises and cold spots. A brief smell of perfume has also been described in some of the accounts, as well as footsteps in the empty hall, doors opening and closing, and lights that turn themselves on and off.

Whoever the ghost (or ghosts) may be, they apparently enjoy music. In addition to the voices heard singing on tape, a story is told of how one student heard a piano playing in one of the rooms in Messick. When he approached the room, the playing stopped and he found that the room was empty. As he turned to leave, he closed the door behind him, and almost immediately the music resumed. Opening the door, he once again found the room empty and quiet.

"Oh, yes, there's definitely something here," Reid Parker, the Design and Production technical director states. "I haven't heard any unusual music, but there have been times when I've been working here late at night, and I *know* I'm the only one in the building. But I'll still here doors opening and closing, and occasionally what sounds like footsteps."

Jeni Parker, Reid's wife and a scenic designer/stage manager for the department, agrees that there's more ghostly drama in the building than what can be seen on stage. "There have been quite a few good stories of the ghosts here in the theater over the past few years."

Perhaps one of the strangest stories involved a man who had brought his two dogs with him into the auditorium building. He had carried them in with him in his arms, and when he entered a certain room, the dogs began to bark and whimper. They jumped out of his arms, ran wildly for a few seconds, and then dashed out of the room. When he tried to take them back, they would not go in. No matter how much the owner persisted, the dogs refused to enter the room.

Neither Reid or Jeni seem concerned about sharing their theater space with otherworldly residents. In the world of theatre, that's only to be expected. Others, however, are not quite as comfortable with the idea.

Delta Childers, the costume shop supervisor, has often gotten an eerie feeling when she has walked through the basement hallways surrounding the costume shop. And many students are apparently reluctant to be in the basement area alone at night.

In spite of the eerie feelings, the Messick building and its predecessor, the Model School, have served the students of ECU well for many years. If the ghost there is indeed that of the poor student whose dream of being lead in the school play was never realized in life, perhaps the building is giving service to that one student still.

THE PAUL GREEN
THEATER/CENTER
FOR DRAMATIC ART

THE UNIVERSITY OF NORTH
CAROLINA AT CHAPEL HILL

> Oddly-colored apparitions and other ghostly activities have been reported at this fairly recent addition to the university campus, situated just next to an old town cemetery.

The University of North Carolina-Chapel Hill has long been considered one of the most beautiful college campuses in North America, and rightfully so. The 729-acre campus is awash with colorful flowers, old oak trees, and striking architecture on buildings that span two centuries. As a student and later Stage Properties Manager working in the Department of Dramatic Art at UNC, I have always been glad to spend time on the historic campus as part of the university community.

In addition to being one of the most beautiful schools, it is also one of the oldest. Founded in 1789 as the first state-supported university in America, the school has produced such notable alumni as actor Andy Griffith, Pulitzer Prize winning playwright Paul Green, and news commentator Charles Kuralt. Both Paul Green and Charles Kuralt are

The Paul Green Theatre/Center for Dramatic Art. *Photo courtesy of the author.*

buried in the Old Chapel Hill Cemetery located at the northwest entrance of the university.

Standing next to the wooded cemetery is the university's Center for Dramatic Art, home to the theater that bears the famous playwright's name. Constructed in 1978, the Center produces a wide variety of theatrical productions, and contains not only the Paul Green, but also a second theater space (the Elizabeth Kenan) for the student-run LAB! Theater; costume and scenic shops; multiple classrooms and workshop spaces; and administrative offices. The Paul Green Theater is home to Playmakers Repertory Company, a professional theater-in-residence that features visiting actors, directors, and designers as well as students currently studying in the Department of Dramatic Art.

It is also apparently home to at least one resident ghost, and probably more. Students, faculty, and staff alike have reported strange apparitions and sounds since the building was first put into service. One source claims that the theater's spectral residents are the ghosts of Confederate soldiers, although there appears to be no substantial evidence to support this. The same source goes on to state that "a woman…who was studying for final exams in the Paul Green Theater…looked up from her books, and there was this shade of a person. In appearance it was unsubstantial…and she knew all of a sudden this person was spirit. She looked at him for a while, and he didn't say anything. Then she asked him…if he was in purgatory and needed her prayers. Then she said the visitation vanished."[1]

Somewhat vague, this re-telling of an old account offers no further information—no names, no dates, not even a good description of the supposed "apparition." Another story, however, seems to mesh nicely with what recent past and present students and employees already know.

Paul Green's gravesite in the Old Chapel Hill Cemetery, located next to the Center for Dramatic Art. *Photo courtesy of the author.*

According to author Daniel Barefoot (himself a UNC alumnus), when the theater was first opened it "quickly became haunted by one of the old university's newest ghosts. No one is quite sure who or what it is. Eyewitnesses have described the thing as a fuzzy green light. It has most often been seen between the shop and the main performance hall. At other times, the eerie ectoplasm has been sighted at the stage left portion of the auditorium. It appears to have the height of a normal human being."[2]

McKay Coble, the Dean for the Department of Dramatic Art, has often seen this strange apparition, usually during play rehearsals. "I first saw it about 10 or 15 years ago, just out of the corner of my eye, in the upper house right (stage left) of the theater. It was the size and shape of a man, and was a pale greenish-yellow." Dean Coble goes on to state that there will be periods of a year or so where the apparition disappears and is not seen for a while, but it has always returned. She reported seeing it most recently during a production in the theater in March 2007.

Although I myself have not personally seen the apparition, I *have* gotten some interesting photos in the theater, in areas where the "ghost" is most often reported. And oddly-colored apparitions are not the only unusual things seen (and heard!) in and around the Paul Green Theater. In my work as Stage Properties Manager for Playmakers, I well remember several other odd "happenings" that took place in the theater.

During a rehearsal for a production of *Romeo and Juliet,* I had gone to one of our props storage closets (located just to the right of the theater auditorium) to retrieve a plastic wine bottle. On my way back to the main stage area, about midway up the right hand entranceway, it suddenly both felt and sounded as if someone had blown into the bottle I

A striking "light anomaly" in the house right section of the Paul Green Theater. Is this the theater ghost, or simply a speck of dust? *Photo courtesy of the author.*

was carrying. The sensation was strong enough to take me by surprise, and I stopped for moment to study the bottle. After a few moments' thought, it occurred to me that I had probably just been swinging the bottle hard enough to force air through the neck opening and cause the sound, and tried a few experimental swings to see if I could duplicate it. No matter how hard I tried, however, I couldn't recreate the sound, and only ever heard it that one time.

Another incident took place in front of multiple witnesses. During one night of rehearsal for *Crimes of the Heart,* I was sitting by myself in the house right section of the auditorium, with other members of the cast and crew scattered throughout the theater. From my perspective at one point during the rehearsal, it looked as if a small object came suddenly whizzing out of the house from behind me, and struck something on the set below with a sharp crack.

Regardless of what actually caused the sound, there was no doubt that everyone in the theater heard it. Rehearsal came to a halt, and several members of the crew, myself included, roamed and inspected the stage and lighting grid, looking for anything that could have caused the sound and making sure there was nothing unsafe on stage. Everything seemed to be normal, and we returned to our seats with more than one person only half-joking that it must have been the theater ghost.

"So," the production manager stated as we prepared to get rehearsal under way again, "you all heard that, right?"

Later, it was determined by the scenic artists that a tree branch used in the set had probably split and caused the noise—but they didn't seem one hundred per cent certain. And while the small object I saw could very likely have been a moth or other insect caught in the stage lights, I'm not one hundred percent certain either.

Other strange noises and sensations have occurred in various parts of the theater. One former artistic director for Playmakers always felt very uneasy in a backstage breezeway stairwell, and stated that one night he was certain he heard footsteps following him down the stairs when there was no one else in the building. Dean Coble confirmed that there was rumored to be a "not so nice ghost" in this area, but was uncertain of the exact story surrounding it. I always felt a little uneasy in this stairway myself, although that may have just been the atmosphere of the place at work. In addition to its reputation of being home to a "bad" ghost, it also led to the darkened basement/trap door area of the theater, and always felt slightly damp and cold. I did, however, get one very interesting photo of an unusual "light anomaly" in the stairway. While most "orbs," as they are called, can easily be explained by moisture or dust motes caught in the camera flash, this one had an odd shape, and it seemed interesting that it was photographed in an area long thought to be haunted.

Although no one can say for certain who Paul Green's ghosts may be—Confederate soldiers, "visitors" from the neighboring graveyard, perhaps even Paul Green himself—their presence lends a sense of history to this newest theater on the old campus. Perhaps the graveyard's "residents" next door simply wish to stop by and take in a play every now and then!

A second unusual light anomaly caught in a backstage stairwell. *Photo courtesy of the author.*

Detail of the previous photograph. *Photo courtesy of the author.*

OLD PLAYMAKERS THEATRE (SMITH HALL)

UNIVERSITY OF NORTH CAROLINA AT CHAPEL HILL

> While a number of historical anecdotes relate to this grand old theater, none of them tell the tale of any ghosts there. Yet it seems a former drama department faculty member may have once paid it a visit.

f ever a theater would be haunted based on architecture and history alone, Old Playmaker's Theatre, the fourth oldest building on the UNC campus, most certainly should be. Built in 1851 in the Greek Revival Style, this National Historic Landmark strongly resembles an ancient Hellenic temple, and is the perfect setting for many a theatrical production. Renowned New York architect Alexander Jackson Davis designed the building in this classic style, although he replaced the traditional acanthus leaves at the top of the Corinthian columns with wheat and corn, for a uniquely American touch.

Originally constructed as a combination library and (oddly enough!) a ballroom, the building was first named for former Revolutionary War general Benjamin Smith, in tribute to his generous contribution of land to the university in 1789. The reason for this unlikely combination was actually quite

Old Playmakers Theatre, formerly Smith Hall. *Photo courtesy of the author.*

logical; although the students wanted a ballroom for social events, the university knew that such a trivial use of school facilities would draw objections from its benefactors. So while the building was used a library during the day, at night on special occasions, the bookcases were rolled back and the hall was used as a ballroom. The front portico of the building faces east, in welcome to distinguished guests coming from the state capitol of Raleigh.

Smith Hall remained the university's library until the early 1900s, although its use as such was briefly suspended during the Civil War when (a popular campus legend states) it was converted to a stable for the horses of the Michigan Ninth Cavalry. In 1907, the School of Law took up residence in the building, complete with (another unlikely combination!) a campus bathhouse in the basement! Finally, in 1925, Smith Hall was remodeled for use by the Carolina Playmakers and renamed the Playmakers Theatre, making it the first building ever on a state campus university to be devoted to the Dramatic Arts. It has been used as a theater by the University's

Department of Dramatic Art until only recently, when the building was temporarily closed for much-needed repairs.

It *should* be haunted. Yet despite its rich and colorful history and strong theatrical tradition, not a single ghost story or spooky campus legend could be found in connection to the old building. Exhaustive research, both on the Internet and in the university's libraries, turned up nothing, nor did interviews with faculty/staff, alumni, and students. For my part, I will admit that in all my years as a drama student working on productions in Playmakers Theatre, I never once experienced anything in the building remotely out of the ordinary.

However...

A chance conversation with one of my coworkers at Playmakers gave me this previously unheard tale. Eric McKetchum, current Student Director for the LAB! Theater at UNC-CH, tells this story about his experience at Old Playmakers when he was a student:

"I was working on a set in the theater over Spring Break in '99. Most of the students were gone, but there were still visitors roaming the campus, and occasionally one or two would wander in wanting to see the old theater. I would tell them it was fine with me, and continue my work.

The dedication plaque on the front of Old Playmakers. *Photo courtesy of the author.*

"At one point, I happened to glance up, and saw an older-looking man in a brown tweed jacket looking down at me from the sound booth. I didn't remember seeing him come in, so I called up to him and got no answer. I started towards the stairs leading up to the sound booth—no one passed me coming down, and when I got to the booth itself, there was no one there. I have to admit, I was a little shaken by the whole thing and felt uneasy working in the theater the rest of the day.

"Later, I was walking through the administrative offices of the Center for Dramatic Art (which houses the Department of Dramatic Art at UNC), and happened upon a portrait of Professor Fred Koch, one of the early faculty for the department. It was the man I had seen in Playmakers, right down to the tweed jacket."

Professor Frederick Henry Koch was the founder of the Carolina Playmakers, and passed away in 1944. Perhaps, like a proud parent, he was simply checking in on "his" theater, and was hopefully glad to see that even many years later the old building still carries on its tradition as a home to the dramatic arts at UNC.

The light booth at Old Playmakers. Could the ghost of Professor Koch be in residence here? *Photo courtesy of the author.*

MEMORIAL HALL

UNIVERSITY OF NORTH CAROLINA AT CHAPEL HILL

A man in period clothing has often been seen in this campus building once known as "The Coffin."

et another theater on the UNC campus rumored to be haunted is Memorial Hall. Located less than half a mile down the street from Old Playmakers Theatre, Memorial Hall serves as both an auditorium for university functions and a theatre performance space for school groups and visiting artists alike. It has hosted such notable performers as actor (and UNC alumnus) Andy Griffith, singer James Taylor, and comedian Graham Chapman of *Monty Python* fame.

First constructed in 1885 to hold the overflowing crowds for that year's commencement, the original hall served the University community for many years until it became unsafe for use, and was demolished in 1930. The current building was completed in 1931, with the original cornerstone installed at the easternmost column of the hall's front portico. In addition to its function as a theater and auditorium, it also serves as a memorial to UNC faculty, staff, and students who died in the line of duty, as well as to other notable alumni. One such alumnus is David Lowry Swain, who served as university president from 1835 to 1868 and North

Carolina governor from 1831 to 1835. Various plaques lining the walls of the building, both inside and out, are dedicated to him and the memory of other distinguished North Carolinians.

While Memorial Hall has several full-time staff members that see to the day-to-day operations of the building, the technical aspects of the functions there—loading touring shows in and out, setting up for lectures and concerts, etc.—are most often handled by student employees. I worked at Memorial Hall myself as a stage lighting technician during my student days at the university, and it wasn't long before I began to hear the stories of Memorial's "ghost."

There was rumor that someone in years past had fallen down one of the staircases in the auditorium and died from the fall, and many seemed to believe that it must be his ghost who had taken up residence in the building. I never saw any actual sight of the Hall's spectral resident, but I do well remember that there seemed to be a perpetual "cold spot" in the house right stairwell, present in that area regardless of the time of year or temperature in the rest of the building. I would often encounter this cold spot as I walked these stairs on my way to and from the light booth upstairs, and never failed to get a chill from it. While I admit that this could very well have been due purely to the "power of persuasion," I remember running into and being puzzled by this anomaly even before I knew the story of the stairwell (and in fact, the story doesn't even specify in which stairwell the accident occurred). Other of my fellow employees at the Hall claimed to have experienced it as well.

There was also one incident while I was working at the Hall that was seen by multiple witnesses. During

Memorial Hall. *Photo courtesy of the author.*

The first Memorial Hall building as it appeared in 1885. *Photo from Wikimedia Commons.*

rehearsal for a show, the stage manager on duty commented that the first electric (the first horizontal bar in the fly space that held lighting instruments) was mysteriously moving on its own, and she had no idea what could be pushing on it. I along with most of the other crew members came backstage to see for myself, and sure enough, the first electric was swinging merrily back and forth with apparently nothing there to cause it. The stage manager stated it had been doing that for some time, and it continued for well over half an hour after I had seen it. It was a heavy electric with fixed lighting, not an empty pole for movable instruments, and it seemed unlikely a draft would be strong enough to cause it to move. Not only that, but this had never happened in all the years I had been working at Memorial, and as far as I know, never happened again.

The upper sections of the theater building seemed to be a popular spot for the Hall's resident ghost. My father Jay Lambeth, who had himself been a student at UNC, had often played concerts in Memorial Hall as a member of the University band. He never had any personal contact with the ghost, but he told me that he'd heard several stories from other people who'd had the unnerving experience of taking a seat in the balcony section, only to suddenly feel that someone—or some*thing*—was sitting down in the apparently empty seat next to them.

Like my father, while I myself never actually had personal contact with the ghost, I heard stories from other people that did. Angeli Primlani, a friend and fellow theater technician who worked as a stage manager at Memorial for several years, commented during our time there that she thought she had felt and seen a "presence" in the balcony of the theater. In one of my recent e-mails to her, I mentioned that I was currently working on this project and that it was making me fondly miss our college days; I also asked her if she remembered anything about the ghost at Memorial.

"How weird is this!" Angeli wrote back. "I've [also] been....waxing nostalgic for the Good Old Days when we all did theater together...

"Yeah, Memorial had a ghost. I saw it once, I think. A man in tan or yellowish 1930s clothing who'd sit in the audience up near the light booth. I used to call him Dave and when I'd lock up I'd wave and say G'night, Dave. (No, he never said G'night [back] or anything else for that matter! I'm not even certain I did see him that one time. It was only for a second.) As far as I know, I'm the only one who ever called him Dave."

Angeli actually is not the only person to address Memorial's ghost as "Dave." According to a 2005 article in Carolina's on-line faculty and staff newspaper, the *University Gazette*, other employees at the Hall also knew the ghost by that name. Butch Garris, production manager and long-time employee at Memorial Hall, says his boss called the ghost Dave, and Butch was told that was the name of the person who had fallen down the stairs and died. Garris, however, believes it's more likely the name was taken from David Swain's plaque.

In recent years, though, the ghost's name gradually changed to "Evan" when a student working at the hall developed an ongoing relationship with it. She felt that she could see him sitting in the balcony every time she came in the hall, and described him as "a beat up, bloody—not friendly— fellow, almost like he was looking for help." If this was truly the ghost of a man who had fallen down the stairs, it's little wonder he would appear that way!

A strange-looking man was also seen by Garris' own wife, Erin, sitting plainly in the middle of the theater. "She screamed bloody murder and pointed at him," Garris said, and although he didn't see the man himself, the incident was real and disturbing enough that they called the police to investigate. They too were unable to find any sign of the man in the theater. Her description of the stranger, though, was curiously similar to both the previous student's and Angeli's—a man wearing casual period clothing who seemed like he was trying to get her attention.

Memorial Hall recently underwent major renovations, and re-opened in the fall of 2005 with a grand gala event. Since then, no further sightings of "Evan" have been officially reported, and no other odd incidents appear to have taken place. Many of the spots in the building that Evan seemed to frequent are no longer there, removed during the course of the construction. While rumor has it that a certain seat had been set aside for Evan at performances in the hall, is that still the case now that he apparently no longer is there?

As Butch Garris put it, "The truth is, Evan can sit just about any place he wants."[3]

DANA AUDITORIUM

GUILFORD COLLEGE, GREENSBORO

> The ghost of a soldier called "Lucas" is often seen and heard in the auditorium of this Quaker-founded college.

The city of Greensboro, the third largest in North Carolina, is an area steeped in tradition, history— and haunting. Although the city was not officially incorporated until the early nineteenth century, it nevertheless played a vital role in the history of the country, and continued to do so through the nation's formative years. The city was named for the Revolutionary War Major General Nathanael Greene, who commanded the American forces at the Battle of Guilford Court House on March 15, 1781. Although the Americans lost the battle, Greene's troops inflicted such heavy casualties on the British Army of Lord Cornwallis that the English general was forced to withdraw, and to regroup his men in Yorktown, Virginia.

The British defeat at Yorktown shortly thereafter, winning the war and securing America's independence from Great Britain, was due in large part to the efforts of General Greene and his men. Greensboro later went on to briefly serve as the capital of North Carolina and even of the Confederacy during the Civil War, when the train of Confederate President Jefferson Davis stopped in Greensboro for three days during which time Davis held several staff meetings.

The city also contributed largely to the desegregation movement in the 1960s, when one of its downtown Woolworth's stores was the site of a historic sit-in protest that lasted for several months, eventually leading to the desegregation of this chain of stores and numerous others throughout the country.

Another historical fact that is unique to Greensboro is the area is home to a large Quaker community. Early Quaker settlers had founded the settlement of New Garden in the area prior to the Revolutionary War. The community was eventually absorbed into the city proper when "Greensborough" (as it was spelled then) was set up as

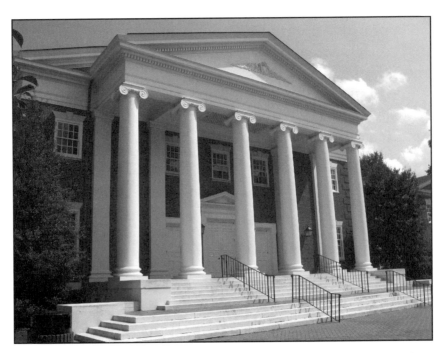

Dana Auditorium. Does the ghost of a soldier named "Lucas" haunt these halls? *Photo courtesy of the author.*

the seat of Guilford County in 1808. Their legacy, however, continues to make an impact on the city even today.

One way in which the Quakers' legacy is evidenced is in the educational institution set up by them. Guilford College is a small, private four-year liberal arts college set in the heart of what was originally the New Garden community. Founded in 1837 as the New Garden Boarding School, the institution later reopened its doors in 1888 as Guilford College when the academic program there was expanded. Today, the college is the third-oldest coeducational institution in the country, and the oldest in the South. It is also the only institution for Quakers founded in the southeastern United States, although only a small percentage of the current student body are Quakers themselves.

Many additions, renovations, and modifications have been made to the college throughout the years, including new classrooms, administrative buildings, and residence halls. One of these additions is Dana Auditorium, a building which houses not only an auditorium but also classrooms and faculty offices. It is one of Guilford College's signature buildings and the home of the Eastern Music Festival, a nationally-known organization that is one of this country's foremost training programs for aspiring young musicians between the ages of fourteen and twenty-two.

Made possible by a donation from educational philanthropist Charles A. Dana, the auditorium was one of three buildings added to the college during campus-wide improvements in the early 1960s. It was constructed on the site of what had been the campus YMCA building first built there in 1891, and serves not only the Festival and the college community, but numerous other annual community programs as well.

And in spite of the building's relatively young age, there are many campus stories and rumors concerning the ghosts of Dana, and how they came to haunt the auditorium. One of the most prevailing stories is that Dana's ghosts are those of the soldiers who died at the Battle of Guilford Courthouse nearby. There is also speculation that the auditorium is built over an old army field hospital that was set up during the Revolutionary War, and that the ghosts are those of soldiers who died there. But while members of the College community may not agree on the actual source of Dana's ghosts, they all agree that *some* presence seems to be there in the auditorium. Numerous stories over the years have been reported of lights switching off and on, odd "cold spots," and in some cases, actual spectral appearances.

One of Dana Auditorium's best-known ghosts appears to be that of a soldier the faculty and students have nicknamed "Lucas." His exploits seem to take place mainly in the choir room of the auditorium and in the Moon Room, a class/meeting space also located in the auditorium building. By most accounts, Lucas has a mischievous but harmless nature. "He likes messing with the locks on closet doors, especially in the choir room," one student commented; another incident involving a door occurred when a college security officer found he couldn't close the door because of what was felt to be a strange force pulling it the other way. There was also an account of where one Public Safety Officer had turned off all the lights in the Moon Room and locked the door; when he came back a little later, someone had turned all the lights back on, although the door was still locked.

"...I unlocked the door, shut out the lights, and said 'Lucas, good night,'" the officer reported.[4]

Lucas's most notable performance, though, is that he apparently enjoys playing on one of the pianos in the choir room. Faculty, staff, and students alike have all reported hearing the sounds of a piano when there is apparently no one there to play it. Security guards at the auditorium have investigated this phenomenon numerous times, but none have ever caught a living person playing.

Piano music in the building is not unique to Lucas, however. Music majors at the college often practice in the auditorium, and this apparently attracts yet another of Dana's resident ghosts. She is reported to be less friendly than Lucas, a "little girl with a malicious streak," although there has been nothing found to indicate who this ghost might be. One music major reported that he had been playing the piano in the choir room late one night, "and this little girl came in and just watched me. It was a little sketchy, so I left." Other students also witnessed the appearance of this apparition during a séance held late one night in the auditorium; she was described as being "a little girl with no face and dark hair in a white dress in the second row."[5]

In addition to the little girl, apparitions thought to be Lucas or his fellow soldiers have also been seen in the auditorium. A tall, thin man in a military uniform of some kind has repeatedly been seen in various locations throughout the auditorium, although the apparition lasts only briefly. There have also been reports that some times, after all the seats in the auditorium have been left folded up in the empty building, one lone seat is seen to be left down, as if someone was sitting in it. Even when there is no apparition to be seen, however, a presence or feeling that there's "someone there" is often felt by those who enter the auditorium.

The most notable story of haunting incidents at the auditorium may or may not be true, as no facts (names, dates, etc.) could be found to back it up; but it is chilling nonetheless. According to the story, two security guards were alone in the main auditorium chamber, over which was mounted a heavy chandelier. The two guards watched in amazement as the chandelier began to swing on its own, finally building up enough momentum to detach from the ceiling and crash to the floor. The incident was apparently attributed to Lucas, although if the other stories are true it would seem more likely to be caused by the ghost of the "malicious" young girl.

Although I myself have never had the opportunity to work on a production at Dana Auditorium, I have attended several concerts and other events there. And while I have never seen "Lucas" or his companions at the auditorium during one of these events, I did have an interesting experience there while I was conducting research for this book.

I had taken several photographs of the outside of the auditorium building, and wandered inside to get some pictures of the interior. It was a beautiful sunny Sunday afternoon, and various students and other passers-by were wandering the campus, although the auditorium itself seemed to be mostly deserted. I had been told I was welcome to look through the auditorium, as long as I didn't disturb some of the classes and meetings taking place there; so I walked through the entrance hall and into the darkened auditorium.

I spent several minutes taking photographs from various angles in the auditorium. I had been vaguely disappointed at the time that there was apparently nothing out of the ordinary in any of my photographs, and remember playfully calling out, "Hi, Lucas, don't mind me; I'm just here to take some pictures of your beautiful theater. If there's anything you'd like to say or do, please do so."

Almost immediately a loud *bang* came crashing out of the back of the theater. I can't describe it; it didn't sound like a door closing or anything falling to the floor, more like two pieces of wood being slammed together. And while it could very likely have been caused by someone or something else outside the building, the timing of the sound along with the creepy feel of the empty darkened auditorium was more than enough to convince me I had taken plenty of pictures, and it was time to go.

Regardless of who the ghosts of Dana may actually be, there seems to be no doubt in the minds of the college community that they are definitely there. As one student put it "...[there has been] a lot of paranormal activity over there. It's definitely haunted."[6]

AYCOCK AUDITORIUM

UNIVERSITY OF NORTH CAROLINA AT GREENSBORO

> A heartbroken woman who lost her fiancé in the Civil War has taken up residence in the theater building that stands on the site of her former home.

In 1891, a North Carolina teacher and women's education advocate named Charles Duncan McIver encouraged the enactment of legislation creating the first state-supported school of higher education for women. One year later, the State Normal and Industrial School opened its doors in Greensboro on October 5, 1892, and provided instruction in business, domestic science, and teaching. Over the years, the school has gone through many name changes, becoming the State Normal and Industrial College in 1896 and later the North Carolina College for Women in 1919. It became part of the University of North Carolina system in 1932 (although still for women only), and finally emerged as the coeducational University of North Carolina at Greensboro with the admission of male students in 1963.

Of all the buildings on the 210-acre campus, one of the oldest and most active is Aycock Auditorium. Constructed in the early 1920s to augment the growing school, the auditorium is located on the site of what was once a private residence at the intersection of Spring Garden and Tate

Streets in Greensboro. The college purchased the land and tore down the original dwelling there to make way for the new theater. And ever since the auditorium first opened its doors in 1926, a ghostly presence has made itself known in the theater.

This is one of those interesting situations where the ghostly inhabitant of one building appears to carry its residence on into the next structure constructed on that site. According to campus tradition, the home that had once stood where Aycock is now was haunted by the ghost of its former owner, a woman who had lived there in the late 1800s. The story goes that as a young woman, she received the sad news that her fiancé had been killed in the Civil War, and she never recovered from the shock. After years of simply going through the motions of life, she finally ended her sad life by hanging herself in the attic of her home. Her ghost was said to haunt the structure from the time of her death until it was taken down by the university.

After the auditorium was completed on the site of her former home, the ghost apparently moved right in to the new building. Almost immediately she began to make her presence known by turning lights off and on and tumbling objects about. Raymond Taylor, a teacher on the campus from 1921 to 1960, had several experiences with the ghost, and recounted them in an old interview.

"She seemed, when I knew her, to delight in the upper reaches of Aycock foyer where she assumed the guise of lights that flitted from ceiling place to ceiling place and dragging chains and clanking objects over the floor down in the lobby up to my office door." Raymond went on to tell the story of how he and a colleague were sitting in his office around midnight when suddenly, the door opened, a blast of cold air came in, and they heard the receding clank of chains. They got up and turned on the lights in the hallway and looked all over, but could never find an explanation for that occurrence.

Over time, as the ghost continued to make herself at home in the theater, the faculty and students there affectionately came to call her "Jane." One student who worked at Aycock in the 1960s on several theatrical productions, noted that Jane could often be counted on to predict the outcome of the most recent production "by making the flies above the stage swing in a circular fashion, as a hanged corpse would swing…if the flies were swinging, we'd have a good performance; if not, well, things wouldn't go very well." For the most part, Jane is considered a friendly, playful, and sometimes helpful ghost, although one with a mischievous streak as well.

Aycock Auditorium, home to "Jane." *Photo courtesy of the author.*

I worked one year with UNC-G's summer theater in 1986 as a member of the costume crew, and remember first hearing the stories of Jane. Many people I worked with that summer told me they had seen the lights go off and on in the theater, and I recall being fascinated that a switch on the auditorium lighting board was actually labeled "Jane's dimmer." I also remember occasionally encountering a "cold spot" in the upstairs balcony; many people felt that the balcony was one of Jane's favorite spots since it was likely the closest location to the attic where she had hanged herself.

One of my coworkers that year also told me she had what she thought was an encounter with Jane: "I was sitting in the balcony watching a rehearsal down on stage, and had my dog with me. Nothing seemed out of place, but every so often my dog would suddenly jump up, run to the opposite side of the balcony, and sit as if waiting for something. Then he would return and lay down for a while, only to jump up and do it again a little while later. I figured he was just playing with Jane." My coworker never actually saw Jane, but that's not to be surprised at; for some reason, while both men and women have witnessed strange incidents credited to Jane, she would only actually reveal herself to men. Up to this time, no female has ever seen her specter in human form.

Jane has, however, appeared to numerous male students and faculty alike. Many of those who have seen her describe her as a woman with light or gray hair and a sweet smile. Jeff Neubauer, a theater major at the university, was locking up the auditorium one night in 1995 with a fellow student when they caught sight of an odd apparition outside the building: "I looked up, and there goes Jane walking by. It was just a very fair-looking woman with light-colored hair. She walked past the window and kept on walking. We couldn't quite figure it out because we knew there was nobody in the building." Neubauer had a later encounter with Jane when he descended into the props storage area in Aycock's basement. As he was leaning down in search of a prop for the current production (which was, interestingly enough, *The Phantom of the Opera*), he felt a hand on his shoulder. He immediately straightened up and swung around, but no one was there. He made his way back to the stage as fast as he could, and although he claims not to be afraid of the ghost, he refuses to go into the basement alone any more.

Another sighting of Jane was reported in 1997. A UNC-G senior who was working on the staging for the musical *Tommy* caught a glimpse of Jane as he began to walk up the basement steps. He had just began to ascend the stairs when he explained, "I saw something in white walking up the stairway into the orchestra pit."

But while most say Jane is harmless, there is apparently a much more frightening aspect to her as well. Veteran theater professor Tom Behm had an unnerving encounter with Jane one evening during a production of *Bye Bye Birdie* that he was directing. Professor Behm had left his briefcase in the theater, and returned to Aycock to retrieve it about half-past eleven one night. When he reached the middle of the darkened auditorium, the auditorium lights came on. Next the stage lights began to flash on and off, and suddenly Behm saw her: "This white kind of apparition, smoke-like thing passed across the stage and came down the steps and was walking toward me...." The professor immediately grabbed his briefcase and left the theater as quickly as he could. He says he has not been inside the theater alone since that night, "...because of the fear of seeing that ghost of Jane Aycock again."

Another frightening encounter took place in front of multiple eyewitnesses. According to one of the spectators there (who confided this story to me on condition of anonymity), "It was when I was in high school, I believe it was around December of 1994, a group of us went there for a classical guitar concert and I was waiting in a small room off the backstage corridor. We all had our guitars sitting in our cases with the lids open and were sitting on the other side of the room from them talking in a little semi-circle. I heard someone run their fingers across one of the guitar strings, looked over and saw a light passing in front of the door, which was closed. I turned back around toward my friends and heard one of the guitar case lids get slammed shut. We all jumped and turned and I saw the same light fading outside the door. I went to the door and there wasn't a soul outside in the hallway and everything was quiet. It really creeped me out. We laughed it off that night, but I really do not like going by that building. Makes all the hairs on my neck stand up."

Stories of Jane continue to be reported even recently. In 2000, Jan Hullihan, then the assistant director for event production at Aycock, was working with a student to set up lights on stage. As they looked up at the high balcony to check the lighting, they saw a figure moving around. "It was like gossamer," she said. "It had this human feel about it. We both saw it. We looked at each other and said, 'Jane.'" They saw the ghostly figure twice more that afternoon, and although they tried to convince themselves there must be a logical explanation, they could think of nothing that would cause such an apparition.

In 2008, a two-year long renovation was completed on Aycock Auditorium that included new seating, better sight lines, additional restrooms, and an improved acoustic quality. The current dressing rooms were expanded, and the existing electrical systems were also upgraded. With the interior completely redone as well, the theater looks practically brand new. But the one thing that hasn't changed at Aycock is Jane's presence.

Two freshmen stage technicians, Ben Pendleton and Taylor Williams, both have stories of their experiences with Jane. Williams was working in the auditorium one evening when she saw a flash of light on the stage. Then she saw the balcony lights flicker. Even after the electricity was shut off, the lights continued to flash. Williams had never heard of Jane before she began work at Aycock, but after her experiences there, she "believe[s] it was Jane to the fullest."

Pendleton had not heard of Jane either, but after he had the feeling of being watched when he was alone in the basement, he began asking questions. He had been in charge of locking the building one night, and tested one particular door to make certain it was secure. After walking on for a moment, he glanced back, and found that the door he had just locked was standing open. And both Williams and Pendleton tell the story of when they left their tools—wrenches, flashlights, gloves—scattered about the auditorium while they worked, and when the two returned to gather their tools, they were found placed neatly in a row.

Jane is definitely an accepted aspect of Aycock Auditorium, and everyone who works in connection with the auditorium is always careful to treat her with respect. Although logically it seems there is nothing to be afraid of, Ben Pendleton best sums up the overall feeling of Jane's presence at Aycock

"I don't think she's a bad ghost. She's fascinating," he stated. "But I won't lock up by myself anymore."[7]

THE CAROLINA THEATRE

GREENSBORO

> The spirit of this beautiful theater has survived in spite of fire and the threat of the wrecking ball. Has another kind of spirit survived here as well?

The Carolina Theatre first opened its doors on Halloween night in 1927 as a 2,200-seat vaudeville theater, and was immediately billed as the "Showplace of the Carolinas." The mayor of Greensboro at that time, Paul Lindley, was issued the first ticket, and joined opening night crowds in admiring the rich architecture of the theater building. Marble columns, classical statues, gilded railings and fixtures, and crystal chandeliers all combined to make the Carolina the finest theater between Atlanta and Washington, D.C. Throughout the course of its career, the Carolina Theatre has hosted a variety of live performances by such notable celebrity entertainers as Vincent Price, Amos and Andy, Tony Bennett, and Garrison Keillor.

The most monumental structure of its type ever built in Greensboro, the Carolina's exterior was just as impressive as the interior. Its terra cotta façade resembled a Greek temple with embellishments painted in rich red, blue, and gold. The floors above the elegant lobby, which were originally intended as business headquarters until the Great Depression struck, are lit by tall windows between the columns.

Inside, uniformed ushers were on hand to greet patrons as they passed through the stately lobby into the equally opulent auditorium beyond. In addition to its striking architectural features, the Carolina Theatre was the first commercial building in the state of North Carolina to be air conditioned. The services and comforts offered by the theater as well as the rich décor both inside and out was designed to provide ordinary citizens with a fantastical experience, affordable even during the Great Depression at seventy-five cents for adults and fifty cents for children.

In its early days, the Theatre's programs featured live performing acts, the *Carolina News* newsreel, the Carolina Theatre Orchestra, audience sing-alongs, and silent films accompanied by the impressive theatre pipe organ. Vaudeville acts routinely made their stop at the Carolina as well. However, vaudeville's days were numbered by the introduction of "talkies"—movies that came with sound—and in 1928, the Carolina Theatre became the first in the state to install the new Vitaphone speakers. Moviegoers from miles around flocked to see the films that were shown five times daily. For the next thirty years, this downtown movie palace was an active part of Greensboro social life. A Saturday morning children's club known as the Circle K Club was introduced at the theatre after World War II, and entertained a generation of local children.

During the late 1960s, however, the growth of suburban retail businesses and neighborhood movie theaters drew citizens away from the heart of downtown Greensboro. The Carolina Theatre began to decline along with the rest of downtown, in spite of renovations made to the theater in an attempt to keep its audiences.

As attendance dwindled, city planners began to look at the theater property for its potential as business parking, and the threatening prospect of demolition became more and more a reality.

As the years went by and the theater fell more and more into disrepair, the city's United Arts Council stepped in to purchase the historic building in an effort to provide for the growing need for centrally located community performance spaces. The Council acquired the building in 1975, and managed to raise enough in monetary, volunteer, and material donations to restore the deteriorating structure. The Carolina Theatre was renovated into a 1,200-seat performing arts center, and reopened in February 1977.

Four years later, the theater was once again in need of repair as an extensive fire ravaged one of the old

The Carolina Theatre. *Photo courtesy of the author.*

stairwells in 1981. The building shut down for a year while the reconstruction process took place, and a few years later the Arts Council stepped in a second time to launch another campaign for further renovations. These included refurbished office spaces and dressing rooms, new sound/lighting equipment and heating and cooling systems, new restrooms, and a second-floor banquet area (The Renaissance Room). In order to make way for the new amenities, seating in the theater was reduced from 1,200 to 1,075. The theater reopened in 1991, and since then has served as the home of such organizations as the Greensboro Ballet, the Community Theatre of Greensboro, the Livestock Players Musical Theatre, Greensboro Youth Symphony and a variety of other local performing arts groups. Civic organizations, businesses, and individuals rent the facility for meetings, seminars, receptions and even weddings.

Although there have been occasional rumors that the Carolina Theatre is haunted, they are purely speculation. A local story alleges that a woman by the name of Melbaline Frye was killed in the 1981 fire, and that perhaps her ghost may have haunted the stairwell, but there is no factual evidence to support this. I spent one summer season at the Carolina Theatre myself as an Assistant Business Manager with the Livestock Players Musical Theatre, and had no odd experiences of my own, nor did I hear any stories while I was there. However, James Fulbright, a former box office manager at the theater, has this story to tell about his experience there in the fall of 1989:

"It was the week before the theatre was going to be closed for renovation, and I along with one other employee were pretty much all that was left of the staff—most of the others had moved on to other jobs. The other employee, Brian, had been working there with me, and we were both finishing up work for the day and getting ready to leave. As I walked towards the back entrance of the house, under the mezzanine through the stage right breezeway, I heard what I thought was Brian saying to me, "Good night, James." I replied, "Good night, Brian," and continued on to the parking lot outside—only to realize that Brian's car was nowhere in the lot, and he had apparently already left the building before I got outside. I even went back and circled around the theater to be sure he hadn't parked elsewhere, but didn't see his car anywhere else. The theater had been completely empty—we were the only two left in the building at that point—and I have no idea who it was that could have spoken to me."

"Melbaline's" staircase was removed during the ensuing renovations, and there have been no reports of any odd activity there since. The Carolina Theatre, however, continues to have plenty of spirit even if it's not of the ghostly kind! A statement from the Halloween 1927 opening night flyer puts it best

"The Carolina Theatre represents, to you and to us, far more than a structure of brick and stone, far more than a prideful addition to the city's importance. It represents a magnificent edifice which we hereby entrust to your care and which we have sincerely dedicated to the pleasant task of rending life more cheerful. If we succeed in spreading happiness to you and yours in the months and years to come, we shall deem our reward sufficient and our vision, our labor and our accomplishment as having been worth the effort."[8]

THE OLD COURT HOUSE THEATRE

CONCORD

> The ghosts of judges and criminals past have been—and apparently still are—seen in the old court house that once served as this theatre company's first home, while "The Deacon" still presides at the church that houses it now.

The Old Court House Theatre company has the unique distinction of having been resident in not just one, but *two* haunted buildings, neither of which were originally constructed as a theater performance space. The first building that housed the company was the Cabarrus County Court House, from which it got its name; the second is a church building originally home to the First Baptist Church of Concord, where the company currently resides.

Originally constructed of handmade bricks in 1876, the Cabarrus County Court House (the third to be built) replaced an earlier structure that had burned, and served the city of Concord and the surrounding county for nearly a century. It was scheduled for demolition in 1975, until Historic Cabarrus Inc., a group founded to promote and preserve the history of Cabarrus County, went before the county commissioners to ask for a reprieve for the historic building. The Commissioners granted the organization six months to determine a use for the building, and to raise money for its preservation.

Almost immediately, plans were set into motion that assisted in the preservation of the old building. In 1976, a lady by the name of Mary Boger set up a meeting at the Hotel Concord for any one interested in forming a community theater in the county. There had previously been one performing company, The Concord Little Theatre, that had been active during the 1950s, but it had long since become inactive. Mrs. Boger planned for approximately twenty-five people, but by the time the meeting was over, more than seventy people had attended, and had each contributed five dollars towards fulfilling her dream. In her subsequent search for a performance space, Mrs. Boger joined with Historic Cabarrus, and as part of their effort to save the old courthouse, she was granted the use of the second floor courtroom for the theater. At this point, the Old Courthouse Theatre was formed.

From that point on, Mrs. Boger was instrumental in bringing to life a variety of productions, to prove to the community that her group was serious and that local talent could be utilized. She also wanted to show the potential of the old courthouse building. Supporting membership grew to over 200, proving that the citizens of Cabarrus County were indeed very open to the idea of live theater in their community.

As the theater company grew, so did efforts to renovate the old courthouse. Another Historic Cabarrus member by the name of Robert Burrage made repeated appeals to the county commissioners, and spearheaded fund-raising drives to bring in thousands of dollars as well as donations of time and materials from local citizens. Volunteers worked hard to clean, paint, and

The historic Cabarrus County Courthouse, first home to the Old Courthouse Theatre company. *Photo courtesy of the author.*

make repairs to the historic structure, and The Old Courthouse Theatre company was credited by many as the driving force that rescued the old building from demolition.

However, in spite of the time and effort put in to restoring the courthouse, it wasn't long before it was in need of more renovations. The ceiling fell in during a rehearsal in the company's fifth season, and temporary repairs were made so that the play could open on schedule. At that point, though, it was discovered that the building was in need of far more extensive work than the theater company could reasonably raise funds for; and the company reluctantly agreed to move from the Historic Courthouse and look for a new home.

That was the end of the Old Courthouse Theatre company's residence in the historic building, but it wasn't the end of the building itself. Historic Cabarrus Inc. continued in its efforts to save the failing structure, and was eventually able to acquire it and turn it into a museum. It now houses (among other things) the Cabarrus County Veterans Museum, dedicated to honoring the county's servicemen from WWI to the present day. And while the Old Courthouse Theatre company never gave any indication of being bothered by paranormal activity, there is apparently more than one ghost from the courthouse's past that still hangs out in the old building.

One of these ghosts is reputed to be that of a young girl named Annabel, whose father was a lawyer with an office in the courthouse. She often enjoyed coming to the courthouse with him when he came in to work, and would play in the bell tower until the sad day she fell to her death from the tower window. Her ghost can apparently still be seen in the window there.

Another courthouse ghost is said to be that of one of its former judges. During renovations on the building (while it was closed to the public), one of the construction workers claimed to have seen a man in a black robe walking down the hallway of the empty building. When the worker went closer to find out who the trespasser was, the man disappeared.

Finally, a third ghost is thought to be that of a man who was wrongly convicted of murder at a trial held in the courthouse, and who had been executed for the crime. He apparently roams the halls in a top hat and long black coat, still maintaining his innocence.

Even though there seem to be no records of the theatre company reporting ghostly activity during their stay in the building, the theatre and the ghosts are still very strongly connected. If not for the efforts of the Old Courthouse Theatre company, it is very likely this building—and its ghosts—would not be around today.

As for the company itself, upon leaving the court house building, they presented a petition in 1984 for re-zoning of the First Baptist Church property in Concord. The First Baptist congregation was moving to new facilities, and the theatre company asked for an option to buy the building. The church building would give them all the space needed for a stage, dressing area, auditorium, and office space with minimal renovation. The city Planning and Zoning Board approved the request, and the Historic District Commission gave their approval. First Baptist agreed to sell the building to the theatre company later that same year.

Constructed in 1922, the current First Baptist Church building stands on the site of another church of the same name dating from 1889. The original structure was demolished in the early 1920s to make way for a new and larger building for the church's growing congregation. And like the old courthouse building, the church has its share of ghosts from its past.

The most infamous of the building's spectral residents is one known as "The Deacon." According to local lore, one of the leading aldermen from the original First Baptist Church died in the influenza epidemic after World War I, and has supposedly remained on the site ever since. He reportedly would turn lights on and off, move hymnals, and even play the pipe organ in the old church. When the first structure was torn down, the congregation thought that perhaps this would persuade "The Deacon" to move on, but apparently he was content to take up residence in the new church building. He continued to play with the hymnals and lights, and would even unlock the doors.

When the church sold the building to the Old Courthouse Theatre company, "The Deacon" went right along with it. The transition gave "The Deacon" a whole new set of elements to work with, and he apparently moves props and other items as well as continuing to play with the lights. He has occasionally been seen as a dark figure lurking in the balcony of the old sanctuary. And like many other church/theatre ghosts, he seems to enjoy music. Singing has been heard in the otherwise empty building, and it is also considered good luck to sing to "The Deacon" while in the old church; it seems to calm down the paranormal activity.

Apparently "The Deacon's" activities have been forceful enough to convince even non-believers of

his existence. One story tells of how a worker at the theatre who didn't believe in ghosts often teased the others there for believing in them, until the night he had a run-in with "The Deacon" himself. The skeptic was working alone in the theatre late one night, on the lights at the control desk, when he heard a noise downstairs in the shop. He ignored it the first time. The second time, however, was much louder, and the worker ran downstairs to the shop thinking that someone had broken into the building. When he got there, no one was around, and nothing in the shop had been moved; there seemed to be nothing there that could have caused the sound. He then called out "Deacon, I am leaving. I'm going to turn off the lights. The place is yours!"[9]

Other ghosts have been reported in addition to "The Deacon." A woman in white has apparently been seen several times in the building; she is thought to possibly be the ghost of a lady whose personal items were donated to the theater company after her death. There have also been accounts of various other ghostly activities such as the sound of keys jingling, and even one story of a messy classroom that mysteriously cleaned itself overnight.

While there may be numerous ghostly occupants in the building, it is clearly "The Deacon" who is undoubtedly the "main player" in the Old Courthouse Theatre's ghostly drama, keeping an eye on the church that has been his home for almost 100 years.

THALIAN HALL

WILMINGTON

> The spirits of several past performers have often
> been seen and felt at this historic performing arts center
> that shares the building with the City Hall.

The Thalian Hall Center for the Performing Arts has
long had the unique distinction of serving as both a
cultural and political center for the city of Wilmington.
Constructed in 1858, its striking architecture was the product of
John Montague Trimble, one of America's leading nineteenth
century theater architects, and its style and splendor have
been copied in numerous other theater buildings since. The
name "Thalian" came from the Greek goddess Thalia, muse
of comedy and poetry.

Wilmington in the mid-1880s was fast becoming a booming
and prosperous port city, experiencing rapid growth and
prosperity. The city fathers felt that a multi-use facility to
accommodate both administrative and cultural affairs was
needed in the expanding city. Consequently, in 1855 the Town
of Wilmington collaborated with the 4th Thalian Association
(an amateur civic theatre company) to begin construction
on the hall. The new building was created to house the city
library and town government offices, as well as a luxurious
1,000-seat "opera house." Wilmington had long been a center
of theatrical activity, both professional and amateur, and the
Thalian Association wanted the facility to be grand enough

Thalian Hall. *Photo courtesy of the author.*

to attract celebrities and other noteworthy acts. With the completion of the new opera house, Wilmington did indeed become a major stop on the theatrical tour circuit that included Charleston, Richmond, and New Orleans.

The hall officially opened on October 12, 1858, with a company from Charleston presenting a popular romantic drama. One of the evening's highlights was the unrolling of a beautifully painted stage curtain that graced the stage for many years, and is even now still on display in what was once the theater lobby. Although performances by the Thalian Association were well received over the next few years, the company was unable to make enough money to cover its expenses, and in 1860, the Association gave the theater over to the Town of Wilmington.

In the years that followed, Thalian Hall played host to a number of notable artists and other visiting dignitaries. Some of these include Buffalo Bill Cody, Maurice Barrymore, John

Interior of Thalian Hall, showing the beautiful period architecture. *Photo courtesy of the author.*

Phillip Sousa, and Oscar Wilde. The theater also hosted a wide variety of community events including concerts, graduations, exhibitions, and even roller-skating! The Hall continued to present touring events along with productions by local repertory companies through the end of the 1920s; but at that point, the great days of touring road shows were coming to an end, with the last of these performances being given by the Ziegfeld Follies in 1928. In 1929, a new local theatre group was organized which revived the old name of The Thalian Association, making it the 5th (and most recent) group of that name. The new company immediately began an annual series of theatrical productions which continue to this day. They have since been joined by a number of newer civic theatre companies that also present comedies, drama, and musicals in the hall. After numerous renovations and name changes (from "Opera House" in 1858 to "Academy of Music" in 1902 and finally to "Thalian Hall" in 1932), the Thalian Hall Center for the Performing Arts now serves over thirty local arts groups, educational institutions, and civic organizations.

Although the old touring road shows may have long been gone from the theater building, some of their members apparently have stayed on. Thalian Hall is reputed to be haunted by several ghosts believed to be those of previous performers, and they are thought to be responsible for quite a few unusual activities that take place in the old building. The hall has its share of "cold spots" and eerie sounds such as the echo of disembodied voices, and occasionally items such as tools, scripts, etc. will mysteriously move from place to place or go missing. Numerous reports have also been made of sightings involving two men and a woman in nineteenth-century dress wandering the first balcony during rehearsals or performances. Their presence has also been felt on the third floor of the theater, along with more "cold spots" and a general sense of uneasiness in this area.

The original painted stage curtain of the hall, now on display in the theater's former lobby space. *Photo courtesy of the author.*

At least two of these specters are believed to be the spirits of actors who both performed at the theater, although not in the same production. The lady is thought to be an actress by the name of Maude Adams, who appeared at Thalian Hall in 1912 as the leading lady in James M. Barrie's *The Little Minister.* The play had been adapted especially for her, and "Maudie" (as she was known to her fans) had an extremely successful run with this play and numerous others both on Broadway and on the road. After a long and prosperous career, Maude Adams died in 1953 at the age of eighty at her summer home in Tannersville, New York. It seems strange that she would come back to haunt Thalian Hall; but perhaps now, as in life, Thalian Hall is but one of many stops "on the road" as she returns to those times and places she most greatly enjoyed in life.

Those who have seen Maude describe her as walking around in a black dress with a big bustle. (According to one box office employee I spoke with, a female figure in white has also been seen, and referred to as "The Gossamer Lady;" but whether this is Maude or yet another phantom form is uncertain). Maude is often thought of as the protector or "guardian angel" of Thalian Hall. A portrait of her in her role from *The Little Minister* hung at one time on the third floor; perhaps that is why her presence has often been felt there.

One of the male ghosts seen at the theater is believed to be that of James O'Neill, an actor and father of playwright Eugene O'Neill. During his day, James O'Neill was considered a promising performer, quickly working his way up the ranks to become a matinee idol. Early on in his career, he portrayed the title character in a stage adaptation of *The Count of Monte Cristo*, a role he played thousands of times with great commercial success. It was this role that he performed at Thalian Hall in 1902, and a photo of him from this production had also been on display in the theater. He died at the age of seventy-two at

his family home in Connecticut; but like Maude, perhaps he simply wishes to visit one of the scenes of his many successes. His ghost is thought to be playfully mischievous, responsible for hiding objects and playing with the stage lights. He is most often reported as being seen seated on the third floor, wearing a dark suit.

Yet another interesting occurrence in Thalian's history took place that may or may not explain some of the building's paranormal activity. During the course of renovations at the hall in 1988, the discovery of skeletal remains under the Thalian floor touched off a flurry of speculation about who they might have been and whether or not the haunting could be attributable to them. Thalian Hall is built on what was once a sand dune, and the pre-Columbian Native Americans in that area buried their dead in the sand; stories of hauntings occurring on the sites of old burial grounds are well known.

In 1990, the hall underwent another major renovation effort, with additional footage added to the original building. Today, the lobby is where the back of the building was at one time, although the grand former lobby still stands at the entrance to the theater auditorium. The new additions to the building house the box office, dressing rooms, the Studio Theater, and administration offices. The Hall also continues in its function as a civic administration building, serving as the principal office of the municipal government.

Now listed with the National Register for Historic Places, Thalian Hall has recently celebrated its 150th anniversary, with plans underway for further improvements to the theater. While the building's technical systems will be upgraded, many of the historical architectural features will be restored to their original appearance. It is to be hoped that Maude Adams, John O'Neill, and Thalian's other resident ghosts will be pleased to see the hall well cared for and returned to its original splendor.

THE CAROLINA THEATRE

CHARLOTTE

> Although the fate of the former grand movie palace is uncertain, there is still plenty of activity at this "little tea party with all sorts of guests."

As one of the oldest cities in North Carolina (and currently the largest), Charlotte, the seat of Mecklenburg County, has a long history of leading the state in a multitude of venues. Founded in 1768, the city was named after Queen Charlotte, wife of England's King George III, in hopes of winning favor with the British monarch. In spite of this show of loyalty, however, the "Queen City" became a known center of political activism during the Revolutionary War, and in fact signed it's own Mecklenburg Declaration of Independence (known as the "Meck Dec") in 1775, a full year before America's own Declaration. The city has ever since been driven to be a leader for the state, and in fact for much of the southeast, in industries such as banking/finance and sports, and has also more recently been working towards establishing itself as a cultural center with a diverse artistic community.

The Carolina Theatre in Charlotte, one of several in North Carolina to bear that name, was one step towards boosting the cultural standing of the city. While many grand movie palaces began life as a strictly live-performance space, the Carolina was built to showcase both vaudeville shows and movies. Constructed in 1927 in the heart of downtown Charlotte, the theatre was the largest in the city, and boasted a price tag of $750,000. The building included a proscenium stage with a beautiful curtain and ample fly space, an orchestra pit, seating for 1,450, dressing rooms, and striking Spanish-revival-style architecture both inside and out. It also featured the only air conditioner in a public building in Charlotte at that time, giving it the distinction of being the only theatre between Atlanta and New York to be able to "manufacture its own weather."[10]

Known as "The Cathedral to Entertainment," Charlotte's Carolina Theatre was not only the largest in the city, but also the largest theatre of that name during its first season. One of its most unique features was its striking architecture. Its designers wanted the theatre to be one of the most luxurious in the region, and to that end they hired two different architects—a prominent local designer by the name of C.C. Hook, and a New York based architect named R.E. Hall—to implement a beaux-arts entry façade along with the Spanish-Moorish flavor. The entry-way was placed in the middle of other store fronts to make the most of the street frontage; office space above and retail space to the sides brought in more profit than the theater did itself, and it was hoped moviegoers might stop and shop on their way in and out of the theater! The offices were intended for use by film entrepreneurs and corporations; in addition to establishing itself as a leading cultural area, Charlotte also served as the film booking and distribution center for everything between Atlanta and Washington, and it seemed only appropriate to have these offices connected to a grand theater.

Other opulent features in the theater included a stunning wrought-iron box office at the street-level entrance; antiques imported from Spain and Italy; reproductions of famous paintings; and lush velvet draperies. The theater also boasted an impressive Wurlitzer pipe organ, and smart, uniformed ushers who helped patrons to their seats. The building and its services brought a level of luxury that was not seen elsewhere in the area, and it was where much of Charlotte society went to catch the latest in movie and live entertainment.

The theater's grand opening took place on March 7, 1927, and presented the film *A Kiss in a Taxi* starring Bebe Daniels. The opening show cost fifty cents with open seating, and in addition to the movie featured vaudeville acts, a Paramount newsreel, an orchestra overture, and a solo on the pipe organ. Throughout the years, other first-run movies ran with great success, such as *Gone With The Wind* in 1940 and *The Sound of Music* in 1965. (This movie played at the theater for well over a year, and was reported to have been seen by more people than actually lived in Charlotte at the time!). Along with popular motion pictures, the theater also played host to a wide variety of celebrities and entertainers including Bob Hope, Guy Lombardo, and Elvis Presley, as well as community events such as concerts and high school graduations.

Although the run of *The Sound of Music* was a great success for the Carolina Theatre, its timing also marked the beginning of the end for the grand old building. In the early 1960s, the Carolina Theatre had undergone a major renovation to turn it into the Carolinas home of Cinerama, the widescreen three-projector 35 mm film process. The

projection booth was moved from the balcony level to the main floor, and much of the original ornamentation and Spanish décor was sacrificed for a more modern suburban look. One Charlotte resident, Mr. Dallas Richardson, commented in a 1986 interview with R.K. Headly for *Marquee* magazine that "…when they modernized it, [they] took that beautiful box office and put it over on the side with kind of an art deco sort of thing. Oh, it was hideous! It didn't blend with the original interior. They chopped up the interior … put those huge drapes all around the side, and that big curved screen. Cinerama was nice; that big screen was just a thrill to watch, but I would prefer the old theatre the way it was."[11]

Many other Charlotteans apparently felt the same way. After the run of *The Sound of Music,* attendance at the theater steadily declined. It managed to outlast all other uptown movie houses, but even the Carolina could not overcome the changing lifestyle of middle class moviegoers, and in November 1978, the theater closed with its final film being *The Fist of Fury* starring Bruce Lee. As if adding insult to injury, arsonists torched the building in 1980; and the ensuing demolition of the lobby (incorrectly deemed unsafe after the fire) caused the building to lose its listing on the National Register of Historic Places.

Today very little is left of the original theater. An all-brick building behind the vacant lot that used to be the lobby still houses the theater auditorium, and the adjoining second-floor offices, which once housed medical and dental offices, are now empty. The city of Charlotte is still debating whether to allocate funds for the restoration of the old building; it is estimated that almost 16 million dollars would be needed to convert the space into a community performing arts center.

In the meantime, however, community efforts to save the old building have continued, and various events have occasionally taken place in the cleaned-up, if gutted, theater space. Community organizations such as The Metrolina Theatre Organ Society and the Carolina Theatre Preservation Society have hosted numerous performances by local artists to help create interest in the old building, although it remains largely empty and unused. However, even though there are no regular performances taking place in the theater, there is apparently still plenty of activity.

Lighting/effects technician Bill Freeman, who worked at the Carolina for many years, referred to the theatre as "a little tea party with all sorts of guests."[12] One of these "guests" is a presence that Freeman refers to as "Fred." Fred apparently can be very mischievous; lighting malfunctions and broken equipment have all been attributed to him. Freeman also believes he may have seen Fred at one point in the balcony of the theatre, and described him as "...solid, a white man, thirty to fortyish, in a white Oxford shirt."[13] Although the balcony itself was dark, the figure seemed to reflect light from the stage until it stepped back into the shadows and vanished.

Freeman also reports experiencing other unusual activities. Cold spots have been felt throughout the building which he believes may be Fred, although he also gets the impression from one particular cold spot of an old lady in period clothing. It is apparently a common occurrence as well to hear footsteps in other parts of the otherwise empty building, and seats moving in the balcony. There is also an area near the orchestra pit which seems to put forth a "...a very unwelcome feeling. It feels like it could be the ghost of an unhappy musician. There were a lot of hostilities about using canned music when they changed from a live orchestra because many musicians lost their jobs. I don't like being in that area of the theatre."[14]

However, in spite of the eerie feeling of the gutted space and the unusual things that happen there, Freeman and others who have worked in the theatre have never felt uneasy or threatened. As Freeman puts it, "I remember the people who were here."[14] And perhaps the ghosts are remembering the former splendor of the theater, as Dallas Richardson put best: "The thing that really impressed me about the Carolina was in its hey day. It was real showmanship then. You know, the big screen up there, air conditioning ... they'd fade the stage lights in and out, they'd open and close the curtains. They had a pipe organ. Then, Paramount news, a cartoon, a comedy, and then the feature, and they'd fade the house lights in and out. Just the way they operated it; it was first class."[15]

THE LOONIS McGLOHON THEATRE/ SPIRIT SQUARE

CHARLOTTE

> The spirit of Spirit Square may be found in more than just its theatrical productions.

The aptly named Spirit Square, located in the heart of downtown Charlotte, is one of the city's premiere community facilities for the performing arts and arts education. Part of the North Carolina Blumenthal Performing Arts Center, the center takes seriously its commitment to community education, and offers a wide variety of classes and outreach programs. The Spirit Square complex comprises not only two active theater spaces—the Loonis McGlohon and Duke Energy Theatres—but offices, classrooms, and six art galleries as well. Theatre, music, and dance all come alive here.

The building that now houses the Loonis McGlohon Theatre originally began life as the First Baptist Church of Charlotte. Constructed in 1909, the church's most striking features are a Byzantine dome similar to Madison Square Presbyterian Church in New York, and several remarkable stained-glass windows. There had been some concern at the time the structure was built that the acoustics in the sanctuary might not be adequate to hear sermons, but they did work,

Spirit Square, originally the First Baptist Church of Charlotte, and home of the Loonis McGlohon Theatre. *Photo courtesy of the author.*

and quite well. The sermons apparently reverberated throughout the sanctuary, and the sound of the church music filled the space as well.

In the early 1970s, the church congregation relocated to a new home elsewhere in downtown Charlotte, and the city acquired the building. It was initially scheduled for demolition, but a group of community leaders rallied enough support for the old church to save it from destruction. The building was carefully restored to preserve and enhance its unique architectural details, and was eventually renovated into the 720-seat McGlohon Theatre, which opened in 1976. The Theatre, along with the rest of Spirit Square, was added to the Blumenthal Performing Arts Center in 1997.

Today, the theatre offers a wide variety of attractions including both drama and music, carrying on the tradition of its namesake. Loonis McGlohon was a native North Carolinian, a gifted pianist and composer who performed throughout the United States and in numerous countries throughout the world. A graduate of East Carolina University, McGlohon had a long and illustrious career as a radio/television producer as well as a musician and composer. His songs have been recorded and performed by many entertainers including Frank Sinatra, Rosemary Clooney, and Judy Garland. He collaborated with the late Charles Kuralt on a word-and-music tribute to his home state—*North Carolina Is My Home*—and with fellow composer, Alec Wilder, on numerous other songs.

Even though McGlohon could very easily have made an even bigger name for himself in the New York music scene, North Carolina truly *was* his home. He returned there after his travels to become an important civic leader, championing numerous worthy causes in his community. Mr. McGlohon passed away at his home in Charlotte in 2002, and the McGlohon Theatre honors the man known by many as one of Charlotte and North Carolina's musical treasures.

While a great deal is known about Mr. McGlohon and the theater that bears his name, not as much is known about the ghost or ghosts that supposedly haunt it. There have been reports of the sounds of people walking around in the church/theater when the building was closed and no one but an employee or two was present. Other employees have noted that sometimes when they are in the sub basement of the building, they can hear singing above. These both have the sound of residual hauntings—the echo of sounds trapped in the "fabric" of the building from the days when the church congregation gathered and sang in the sanctuary, and that are simply being "replayed." Or perhaps the singers had enjoyed the remarkable acoustics in the church so much that they've returned to enjoy them again!

However, not all the unusual activity in the building can be attributed to a residual haunting. Jeff Weeks, a theater technician who worked briefly at Spirit Square, had this story to tell.

"I was setting up one night in the theater for 'Monday Movie Night,' and was walking towards the elevator so that I could go into the basement and retrieve the equipment I needed. Before I could even get to the elevator, though, I noticed that it had already started on its way up from the basement on its own, and the doors opened for me just as I arrived—I didn't even touch the button to call it. I thought that perhaps someone down below had sent it up, but when I took the elevator down, there was no one else there. I gathered the equipment I needed and walked back to the elevator—once again, it was there waiting for me, and the doors opened for me as I came up to them. I was glad that I didn't have to mess with the doors myself, but it just seemed odd!"

A performance in the McGlohon Theatre is truly beautiful in both sight and sound. With the church's original stained glass windows and the dome overhead, there is a feeling of both the sacred and the secular combined. Between the church's original patrons and the kind-hearted McGlohon, it seems only natural that the spirit of Spirit Square, whomever it may be, would be glad to lend a helping hand.

IMAGINON
THE JOE AND JOAN
MARTIN CENTER

CHARLOTTE

> An unfortunate young woman seems to have found a home in this cheerful performing arts center built especially for the youth of its community.

Although we generally tend to think of haunted buildings, theaters or otherwise, as historic, mysterious, and often ruined structures, that is not always the case. Many times, a brand new building can come complete with its own ghost, as with ImaginOn: The Joe and Joan Martin Center. Completed in 2005, ImaginOn is a creative arts facility geared towards promoting education, learning, and the dramatic arts for the younger members of the Charlotte community.

More than just an area for the performing arts, ImaginOn is a collaboration between the Children's Theater of Charlotte and the Public Library of Charlotte and Mecklenburg County. In addition to two active theater spaces, the building houses a children's library, studio classrooms, interactive exhibits, and a gift shop. Its two theaters—the 250-seat Wachovia Playhouse and the 570-seat McColl Family Theater—are home to the resident Children's Theater as well as hosting productions by the

The front entrance to ImaginOn. The curved wall to the right is made of stone blocks recycled from cemetery monument cuttings. *Photo courtesy of the author.*

touring Tarradiddle Players, numerous guests artists, and other community programs.

"We wanted ImaginOn to be a safe area for children and teenagers to be able to come and express themselves creatively," Lucy Hazlehurst, Literary Manager for the Children's Theater stated. "There are areas here that are only open to those under eighteen, and each of our exhibits and services, such as the library, are geared towards a younger audience. We wanted young people to be able to learn in many ways, and ImaginOn is unique in its approach to artistic education."

The building is unique in its structure as well as in its service. A wide variety of recycled building materials, along with interesting angles and colors, combine with fun displays and interactive exhibits to give ImaginOn a "cool kind of

The Wachovia Playhouse, one of the theatre spaces in ImaginOn. *Photo courtesy of the author.*

energy—kids would walk into this building and know it was for them," Lucy said. The unusual items used in the construction earned ImaginOn a certification from the U.S. Green Building Council, the first structure in Charlotte to gain such recognition. These recycled materials can be found throughout the building—floors made from old tire and tennis shoe rubber, bathroom doors made from detergent bottles, cabinetry of compressed wheat stalks—and even building stones fashioned from the cuttings left over from cemetery monuments.

It is not the recycled scraps of cemetery monuments, however, that drew ImaginOn's ghost to the building. Like the building itself, the ghost is reputed to be fairly new. Many of ImaginOn's staff have reported odd activities and sounds ever since the building was first opened, and it's believed that the ghost may be that of a young woman who died in an accident during the building's construction.

"There's definitely something," Jeff Weeks, one of the Children's Theater technicians, stated as he worked on the stage in the McColl Theater. "I've been here late at night, and have heard the sound of doors opening and closing when I know for a fact I am the only one left in the building. I've also heard the sound of keys dropping, and one night when I was working on stage, every light in the house went completely dark, and then came back up again just as suddenly. That could likely just have been a power surge, but still....there's something."

One interesting item of note about the theaters in ImaginOn is that, unlike most other theaters, no ghost light is left burning on the stages overnight. Both Jeff and Lucy have speculated among themselves if that might be one of the factors provoking the ghostly activity in the theater—after

The McColl Family Theatre, another of ImaginOn's performance areas. *Photo courtesy of the author.*

all, according to theater lore, one of the purposes of a ghost light is to appease any spectral residents with enough light to see by so they won't become angry and pull malicious pranks. Lucy divulged that the ghost light from the Children's Theater's previous home had actually been brought over and was in storage in ImaginOn, but that they had yet to use it. It was bantered about that doing so would bring out the ghost that had been said to haunt the old Children's Theater building, since that building had been demolished to make way for new office space near downtown Charlotte. (It would be interesting to see if the new structures are haunted by the old theater's ghost—but that's a different story!)

Other Children's Theater employees have had their own experiences with ImaginOn's ghost. Amy Holroyd, the Costume Shop Manager, has witnessed several unusual

"Mysteries of the Theatre," one of the interactive displays at ImaginOn. There is certainly plenty of mystery here! *Photo courtesy of the author.*

occurrences since she has been working in the new building. Washing machines in the shop have turned themselves on and off numerous times, and Amy has heard her name called by a disembodied female voice on more than one occasion. There have also been items moved around in the basement, or items that have mysteriously disappeared only to just as mysteriously reappear later on. Amy's husband Jeremy, who also works in the building as head carpenter for the Children's Theatre, has even heard the ghost call out to him asking "Do you need help with that?"

"He immediately replied 'No, thank you,' and got out of the building as quickly as he could," Amy recalled. "In spite of the weird happenings, though, we don't think she's a bad spirit—we believe that she's helpful and not a threat.

"And we all believe that she's here."

Lucy had her own touching story to tell of ImaginOn's spectral resident. While she herself has never experienced anything directly, she has heard the stories, and also believes the ghost to be that of the unfortunate young woman. She tells the story of the day she and Melanie Huggins, then the director of Youth Services, arrived at the building site the day before construction began.

"We had arrived at the parking deck next door to the construction site, and found that it was full of police and other emergency vehicles," Lucy said. "We came to find out that apparently a young woman had been killed in an accident in the garage that day. It may seem odd, but both Melanie and I felt that, as ImaginOn was built to be a safe place for young people, we wanted this poor young woman to feel she had a safe home here, and so we both invited her in."

Lucy paused, then smiled and continued almost shyly. "And the odd things started happening almost at once. I like to think that she really did find a safe home here."

THEATRE CHARLOTTE

CHARLOTTE

> The company's first director may even now be stopping by from time to time to check in on the oldest community theatre in the state.

In the early 1900s, a grassroots effort to support amateur theatrical productions swept the country during and after the First World War. Known as the "Little Theatre Movement," this social development formed in response to the rise of motion pictures as the primary source of American large-scale spectacles, and the subsequent decline of live theater. A wide variety of experimental theater groups and amateur companies nation-wide participated in this reform to bring smaller and more intimate plays to their audiences. The modern-day community theater is a descendant of the Little Theater Movement, with the term "little" referring not only to the size of the theater performance spaces ("black box"), but also to the focus of the plays themselves. Instead of being the enormous melodramas that had been popular in the past, the new style of plays was more psychological and subtle in nature, and led to the rise of such famous playwrights as Arthur Miller (author of *Death of a Salesman*) and Eugene O'Neill (*The Iceman Cometh*).

Women played a large role in the progression of the Little Theatre Movement. Although their efforts were often dismissed by their male counterparts, they still continued to make positive contributions to this social development that had a lasting impact on their respective communities. In 1927, the Charlotte branch of the American Association of University Women became actively involved in the movement, and formed the Charlotte Drama League. They mounted their own amateur theater production, a reading of *Outward Bound,* a year later in the basement auditorium of the downtown Carnegie Library. Shortly thereafter, the group engaged Thomas B. Humble as its first artistic/executive director, and became incorporated under the name of Little Theatre of Charlotte one year later. Under Mr. Humble's direction, the amateur Little Theatre company produced scores of plays in a highly professional manner. The company made the most of its local talent, utilizing the skills of hundreds of Charlotteans both on and behind the stage. Mr. Humble continued to serve as the company's director for thirty-one years with distinguished success.

In its first few years, the Little Theatre of Charlotte continued to produce plays for the Charlotte community in various locations throughout the city until their first (and current) permanent home was completed in 1941. Located on Queens Road in the affluent and historic Myers Park district of Charlotte, the Little Theatre building served as an attractive home for the growing performance group. Small in both performance and audience space, the 220-seat theater was the perfect venue for the "little" plays that were rapidly gaining popularity as a result of the Little Theatre Movement. The company's first production in its new home was the popular comedy *George Washington Slept Here.*

Since then, Theatre Charlotte has presented over several thousand performances of almost 500 mainstage productions, as well as fostered an education outreach program for the school and the community at large. Hundreds of volunteers work annually with the non-professional company both as cast members and as part of the technical crew. I enjoyed working on several productions at the theater as well, first as a lighting technician for *1776,* and later as one of the "Pick-a-Little Ladies" in *The Music Man.*

It was at that point I first heard the tale of Theatre Charlotte's ghost. Although I never saw or heard anything in the building myself, there were several popular stories roaming about of a mysterious man in dated clothing who was often seen in the theater when no one besides theater personnel was supposed to be around. While my time at the theater was many years ago, back in the mid-90s, sightings of this apparition have apparently continued up to the present time. Chris Timmons, the current Technical Director for Theatre Charlotte and the facility manager for the building, told me, "I have heard from several people regarding a man standing in various places throughout the building when there is no one there [although] I have not been with this theatre long and have not experienced anything myself. It is possible that this person...could be Tom Humble." As Theatre Charlotte's first artistic/executive director, it would make sense that Mr. Humble might want to drop by and check in on his theatre company from time to time! Chris went on to say that, "For decades, his picture has hung in the lobby of the theatre. This past summer, the picture was removed to renovate the lobby and has been moved to a different part of the building. Who knows; this may stir things up."

Another possible source of the theater's mysterious occupant stems from the history of the land before the structure was built. The Myers Park neighborhood, where the theater is located, was once wooded farmland, not too far from the grounds of a neighboring plantation; and the land where the theater stands now was originally a slave burial ground. According to Chris, "It is rumored that the bodies [in the burial ground] were dug up and removed before construction started, but one body was never found. It is possible that this person is the man that people have reported seeing…"

As the oldest continually-producing community theatre in North Carolina, Theatre Charlotte continues to promote and carry out the ideals first started by the Little Theatre Movement. It is one of the few community theater companies to have a home built especially for it that it still occupies today—along with either the ghosts of the former residents of the land, or of its earliest director. Its long history, along with the support of the its community and the talents of its volunteer force, have all combined to make Theatre Charlotte one of the most acclaimed non-professional theatre companies in the Southeast.

THE MANOR THEATRE (REGAL MANOR TWIN)

CHARLOTTE

A former manager continues to report for work at this movie theater years after his death, still dressed in the uniform he wore in life.

Although all of the other "haunted theaters" chronicled here are, or were, playhouses built for the performance of live theatrical productions, their younger sister—the movie or cinema house—is quite often just as prone to ghostly activity. One such movie theater is The Manor Theatre, or Regal Manor Twin, Charlotte's oldest movie house, and one of "the jewels of the Queen City."

Constructed in the affluent Myers Park neighborhood in 1947, the Manor was considered to be the most beautiful movie theater in Charlotte at that time. The bathrooms were floored with hand-laid tile, and elaborate plaster work in art-deco styling framed the theater's movie screen. The building was originally created as a single-screen theater, and opened with *The Egg and I* starring Fred MacMurray and Claudette Colbert. Several years later, however, the theater was divided into two screens, and although this renovation made for smaller viewing auditoriums, it created a more intimate space that went nicely with the independent and foreign titles the theater became known for hosting. (One account states that this renovation didn't take place until the late 70s, with the film *Grease* being either the last movie to play on the single screen, or the first to play after the remodeling had been completed, and the theater had reopened in 1979). Today the Manor serves as Charlotte's premiere independent film venue, although it will still occasionally feature carefully-chosen mainline films. Much like its sister "live" theaters, the Manor has had to adapt to changing times and tastes in order to survive.

And also like it's sister theaters, the Manor has its share of ghost stories. "A few years ago, we had a psychic come in and say we had two ghosts, "said Brandy Ray, one of the managers for the theater. "I kind of feel a negative presence in one auditorium—number one—and a positive feeling in number two." Another manager, Ronnie Barlon, agrees. "Definitely number one is scarier than number two," he confirmed. "When I'm working in that auditorium, I will not look up at the projection booth because I'm scared I'll see someone looking back down."

The frightening presence centered around the number one projection booth is thought to be that of a projectionist (or usher, or perhaps a janitor, depending on the source) that hung himself there in the booth. The sound of disembodied sweeping has been heard in that area, and other strange activities have taken place there as well. "The cabinet door in the number one projection booth won't stay shut," Mr. Barlon reported. "You'll shut it, and you know it's shut, and all of a sudden you'll hear *bam!* and it's opened back up."

Other unusual activities have taken place in the upstairs area of the theater. Employees working in the building have often reported the sound of what seems to be a woman's high heels clicking on the floor upstairs, as if they are going towards the bathroom. This upstairs ladies' powder room seems to be a central point for ghostly activity. Cold spots have often been felt there, and supposedly a medium visiting the theater one evening to see a movie related feeling a very strong impression in the powder room of a woman named "Rose." Another account states that an employee reported hearing a woman scream in an upstairs bathroom; when they went to check on the source of the scream, there was no one there. A similar version of this particular tale tells of how one of the theater managers on duty, Anne Keziah, heard an employee scream from the bathroom, and when the manager raced upstairs to check on the employee, she felt a bitterly cold draft pass her on the stairs. She continued to the bathroom to help the shaken employee, who explained, "While I was in the bathroom, someone hit the wall very hard. They were in the powder room."[16] There was no sign of anyone else in the bathroom, and no one had passed down the stairs—the only exit—except for the draft of cold air.

Scott Flowe, another of the theater's managers, agrees that there's something unusual about the upstairs area and the bathroom there. "I've heard whispering in the bathroom when I'm closing, and it's loud enough to where I've gone in and checked it out," he said. "I'll be angry that there are people still in the bathroom when I'm trying to leave, but I'll walk in and there's no one there." He stated that the building's janitors have often told him they also feel there's something in the upstairs area.

Ms. Ray agrees that there seems to be plenty of activity there. "I'll see something walk by out of the corner of my eye," she reported. "I've seen shadows upstairs when I'm by myself that make me feel I'm not alone."

Although it is not known who all the upstairs ghosts may be, another of the Manor's otherworldly residents appears to be that of yet another former employee. During the theater's first year of operation in 1947, one of its managers at that time committed suicide at his home. While his death was not connected to the theater, his working life apparently had strong ties there, so much so that even after his death he appears to still be reporting for work at the theater dressed impeccably in his dinner-jacket uniform. He is most often seen late in the evening; employees have reported that they have seen a white-haired man attired in a dinner jacket wandering in the theater building after the doors have been locked. He appears so real that employees wonder how someone could have been left in the theater after closing; but upon approaching him and asking "May I help you?" he then suddenly vanishes.[17]

Not only does this particular spirit show up for work, but he also seems to continue with the tasks he performed there in life. It is thought to be his ghost who may be responsible for the sweeping heard outside the projection booth. One employee's account tells of how, while manning the projector in the booth during a movie screening, he heard sweeping just outside. Curious as to who could be trying to clean at that time, he stepped outside the booth to look around, and suddenly felt a *bump* on his foot as if someone had pushed a broom against it. The employee heard the sweeping sound continue past him, all the way down the rest of the corridor. If nothing else, at least the theater's ghostly manager seems intent on helping keep his former workplace in good condition!

While all three managers agree that many of the theater's strange activities could likely be explained by its age, they all still feel that there is definitely something unusual there. "You'll hear stuff, but when you hear it you just chalk it up to the building being old, because you don't want to scare yourself," said Mr. Barlon. "But when I hear things, I'll still get out as quickly as I can." Ms. Ray added, "I've worked here for ten years and I still get an eerie feeling."

In spite of—or perhaps even because of—its ghosts, the Manor Theatre is an excellent place to catch an art-house film. It has survived several ownership turnovers, as well as the threat of the wrecking ball as it seemed doomed to extinction by the movie multiplexes. The theater has built its reputation on showing the best of classic, foreign, and independent films, and even though it is not a modern-day theater with multiple amenities, it does have an updated sound system and modern comfortable seating. Much of its historic charm remains intact, however—the hand-laid tile in the powder room is still there, as is some of the elaborate art-deco plaster work around the movie screen, hidden behind the screen draperies. Still there also, apparently, are the ghosts of some of its former employees and patrons, adding to the unique atmosphere of the oldest and longest running movie theater in the city of Charlotte.

THE CAROLINA THEATER

HICKORY

> A disastrous love triangle and the death of a former manager all left their mark on this playhouse-turned-cinema, still in operation as a movie theater today.

The early 1900s were the heyday of vaudeville road shows. Many great touring acts came through the Carolinas, stopping at various grand road houses such as Thalian Hall in Wilmington, the Abbeville Opera House in Abbeville, and the Carolina Theatres in Greensboro and Charlotte. However, with the introduction of the "talkies" in the 1920s, vaudeville and live theater in general began to decline, and many of these opulent old show palaces were converted into movie theaters. The days of these grand movie houses were also short-lived, however; many of these were eventually closed due to lack of business, and quite often demolished completely. Those few theater-turned-movie houses that escaped the wrecking ball were many times converted back into live-theater spaces and/or performing arts centers, but a small handful remained in business as cinema houses, staying open in spite of the general decline of the great movie palaces. One of these is the Carolina Theater in Hickory, nestled in the foothills of the Appalachian Mountains approximately sixty miles north of Charlotte.

The city of Hickory was incorporated in 1870, having originally begun as a small settlement centered around a tavern/post office constructed in the late 1790s. It grew from a minor trading center to a leading manufacturing center for hosiery, textiles, and furniture, and even today is one of the nation's largest suppliers for the furniture industry. The steady growth of the city's population and economy brought with it an increased need for educational and cultural outlets, and several facilities were built in response to this growth. The Carolina Theater, located in downtown Hickory, was one such facility, providing dramatic and/ or comedic entertainment for the citizens of the growing community.

Opening on Christmas Eve, 1932, as a playhouse theater, this particular Carolina Theater joined its sisters across the state in being a grand show palace for the then-popular road shows. It featured a proscenium stage with an orchestra pit and floor seating for 430, as well as several box seats on each side of the auditorium. Balcony seating and a separate upper entrance/exit was provided for minority patrons. A spiral steel staircase to the house right of the stage led to the dressing rooms below, where many of the theater's visiting performers signed their names on the walls.

However—as with many of the other theater houses across the Carolinas—the Carolina Theater fell prey to the decline of the touring shows, and was converted into a movie theater in the 1940s right around the time of World War II. It retained much of its original grandeur, though, and changed very little over the next twenty years as it continued to provide movie entertainment for its patrons.

During the 1960s and 70s, a vast urban development and renewal project throughout the city caused many of Hickory's historic downtown structures to be drastically altered or even demolished completely. The Carolina managed to survive the city-wide renovations, although not without several changes of its own. A metal awning was attached to the upper half of the building, hiding much of the original brick, and a second movie screen was added to the balcony area to create a second-floor viewing theater. The minority entrance was kept in place but used mainly as the emergency exit for that portion of the building, while the lack of first-floor bathrooms was remedied at that time by the conversion of a downstairs utility closet. The theater continued in operation as a cinema house, offering first-run movies.

Today the Carolina operates as a second-run movie theater, and in addition to the feature films, offers special matinees and community group events. It has changed very little since its early days in film, although the exterior metal awning has since been taken down to expose the brick facing. The outline of where the orchestra pit once stood can still be seen on the hardwood floor, and the stage is still in existence, although it is hidden behind the movie screen. Draperies on the walls also hide the old box seats that are still there, although they have been barred off and are not easily accessible, while the floor around the box office is the original marble from the very first days of the theater. The old spiral staircase leading to the dressing rooms, along with dressing rooms themselves—complete with the signatures of the visiting performers still visible on the walls!—are all intact as well. And lastly, one of the Carolina's best amenities—high-backed rocker chairs dating from the theater's first days as a movie house—

can still be found in the downstairs viewing auditorium, providing a comfortable seat for moviegoers.

Michael Sigmon, a former theater employee who was at the Carolina in the late 80s and early 90s, had several good stories to tell of both the theater's history and its ghosts. He worked as an usher, did box office and concession sales, ran the projector, and later served in the capacity of assistant manager. "We never had titles, like assistant manager or anything like that," Michael recalled, "but I was in charge." One of his fondest memories from his days at the theater was of a fellow employee named "Miss Lacy," who at the age of sixteen had started work in the theater box office the day it opened in 1932, and continued there well into the 1980s, the only job she ever had. Michael also tells of how, in addition to many of the original structures still surviving in the old building, old movie posters/billboards showcasing the theater's early films can be found behind the movie screen.

Another story of the theater's history that was legendary among the generations of employees who worked there was from the early days of the building's service as a play house. According to Michael, the story tells of an actress at the theater who was having an affair with a married actor during the run of one of the performances there. When the actor's wife learned of the affair, she came to the theater to confront the "other woman," and one of the two women was killed—shot—by the other. The story is uncertain as to whether the wife killed the actress or the other way around, but either way, the murder is said to have taken place in one of the downstairs dressing rooms. Michael stated that he'd heard people felt the murdered woman's ghost was in the building, but never heard of any specific haunting activity being attributed to her.

However, he did say he always felt very uncomfortable going down the spiral staircase into the former dressing rooms. "When I worked in concessions, we used to have to go down there several times a day to get ice, because that's where our big ice machine was," Michael recalled. "You can still go down there, but it's a very creepy place, so not many people go down there now."

The most "legendary tale" concerning the theater, however, is that of a former office manager who worked at the Carolina shortly after it was converted into a movie house. Michael tells of how the manager died in his office one day, either by his own hand or the victim of a heart attack, and was not found until the following day. Since then, his ghost is said to haunt the office where he died, and Michael confirmed that the room always felt freezing cold. "The office never stays warm, no matter what you do. That room stays so cold; it's just the kind of room where you go in and your hair stands on end. You know something's just not right there."

The former manager apparently also makes his presence known in other ways. Numerous employees throughout the years have reported hearing the office door slam in the empty upstairs, typically between eleven and twelve o'clock at night, just as the theater is closing.

"I used to hear the stories that you would hear the office door slam shut sometimes, but there would be no one up there," Michael said. "I used to think they were just stories—until I actually had it happen to me.

"I'd been working there for a while and was closing—I was there by myself. Typically, I would study; I would go into the box office, because I could keep the door open and be able to watch as people walked by on the street—make sure no one tried to come in without paying. I would usually sit in there and try to study a little bit until the movies were over, then I would go do my thing and close up. And then I would hear the door slam.

"That door had a very distinct sound, I guess because it was one of the original doors—it had a very distinct slam to it. When you're there at eleven o' clock at night and the movies are going and there's no one in the lobby and you hear it slam, when it first happens, your first response is to run up there to see who got to the office, but of course, there's never anyone there."

Michael went on to say that the sound of the slamming door occurred so often and was heard by so many employees that it became routine. "You weren't alarmed by it any more; it happened to many, many people who worked there. Anyone who opened and closed the building could tell you about it."

Michael is clearly proud of the old building, and rightfully so. It is one of the city's historic treasures, one of the few theaters-turned-cinemas that have stayed on as a movie house. "Over the past twenty years, there have been slow times where they probably could have shut it down, but they kept it going," Michael stated. "It's an old building that's got a lot of history to it." The Carolina Theater has served the citizens of Hickory for a long time, and with any luck, the theater—along with one former manager—will continue to do so for a long time to come.

SOUTH
CAROLINA

THE ABBEVILLE
OPERA HOUSE
ABBEVILLE

> The phantom of this opera house has a chair all
> to itself as it continues to enjoy the productions in this
> historic building.

The town of Abbeville is a small, charming settlement
nestled deep in the western Piedmont Hills of South
Carolina, almost forty miles away from the nearest
interstate. In spite of its remote setting—or rather, perhaps
because of it—Abbeville is a well-known weekend get-away
spot for those who enjoy a historic setting and slower pace of
life. Many of the homes and other buildings in this historic
city—once called the "Charleston of the Upcountry"—are
similar to those found in the town a century ago, and just as
many more are original. One such building is the Beaux-Arts
city hall, home to the Abbeville Opera House.

When the Georgia, Carolina, and Northern Railroad first
began running through Abbeville in 1889, the town boomed.
The Beaux-Arts hall and the opera house were completed
in 1908 as an overnight stop for the many vaudeville road
companies making the New York/Atlanta run. Between
1908 and 1913, the citizens of Abbeville enjoyed over 200
performances on the Opera House stage, including those
by such entertainers as the Ziegfeld Follies and Jimmy
Durante.

Abbeville Opera House. *Photo courtesy of the author.*

It was also during this time that moving pictures—silent movies—began to make their appearance, and starting in 1910, audiences at the opera house were enjoying both live theater and motion pictures. With the musicians and live sound effects, the silent pictures still had some of the appeal of live theater. Once "talkies" (movies with sound) became the norm, however, road show productions began to decline. Slowly, the opera house was converted entirely into a movie theater, and no further live theater productions were held there. It remained a movie house until the late 1950s, when it, like so many other grand movie houses of the day, were forced to close due to lack of business.

At that point, much of Abbeville had been hit by a lag in business, and many of its beautiful storefronts and other historic buildings—the opera house included—had fallen into disrepair and disuse. Shortly thereafter, George W. Settles, then the director of the Abbeville County Development Board, collaborated with other community leaders in an attempt to revitalize the town. Settles had been disquieted to see the grand old opera house sitting empty and abandoned, and attempted to make it a movie house again. It was a short-lived effort, but it enabled Settles and his business partner to convince the city leaders that while the building was not designed to be a movie theater, it could still serve its original purpose as a center for artistic expression. He felt that restoring the old opera house was more than just supporting the arts—it was an economic force that could drive the entire downtown business district.

Settles formed a group dedicated to the preservation of legitimate theater in Abbeville and the surrounding upstate South Carolina region. He felt that the best way to convince the citizens of Abbeville to restore the old opera house was to show them the magic of the theater; and so, with his group the Abbeville Community Theater (A.C.T), he staged numerous productions at the Chestnut Street School. Settles continued to spearhead both productions at the school and the effort to restore the old opera house, and in 1968, the Abbeville Opera House reopened as a home for live theatre with a production of Thornton Wilder's *Our Town*.

Soon after its renovation, the Opera House once again began to draw attention to Abbeville; and in 1978, it began a summer theater season. The year after that, a professional opera company took up residence in the theater, and the Abbeville Opera House has been presenting live theater to the Upstate South Carolina region ever since. It is listed on the National Register of Historic Places, and is the official state theater of South Carolina. Today, it is fully restored to its original condition (with only the exception of modern air conditioning and rocking chair seats); it even still uses the same rope-and-pulley fly systems as in 1908, the only theater in South Carolina to still do so.

Yet another of the original fixtures still to be found in the old Opera House is the Negro (Colored) balcony, an area of the second balcony that in the early 1900s had been reserved for African American patrons. It is here that much of the opera house's ghostly activity seems to take place. Today, of course, the balcony is not used for segregating the audience, and in fact has largely been abandoned except for one lone chair. The chair sits there, empty—or not—reserved for and in honor of the opera house's ghost.

There are two different stories as to just who the ghost might be. One story states that the ghost is believed to be that of an African American patron who frequented the opera house. It was rumored that he had been involved in a romantic relationship with a white actress belonging to the opera company, and had been murdered in the balcony by intolerant citizens. Another story states that the ghost is actually that of an actress who came to Abbeville with one of the touring road companies, and died of illness shortly thereafter.

Whomever the opera house's ghost may be, it is apparently quite active. It is said that if the "ghost chair" is moved, "something unexpected will happen during the play. A curtain won't go up or it will fall down in the middle of the play," said Cheri Standridge, executive director of the Greater Abbeville Chamber of Commerce.[18] Strange lights have been reported appearing in the empty balcony, and many times during rehearsals, performers on stage will hear the sound of someone applauding coming from there. One actor stated that during a standing ovation after a performance, he glanced up at the empty second balcony and saw a lady in period dress standing there applauding as well.

With over 100 years behind it, it's only natural the opera house would creak and groan at night. Harder to explain, though, is the sound of applause when there is apparently no one there to cause it. It's good to know that if nothing else, at least the opera house ghosts are still enjoying the show!

POWELL THEATER/ CHESTER LITTLE THEATRE

CHESTER

A spectacular number of eerie sights and sounds have been reported in this building that is reputed to stand on the site of the city gallows, as well as being the scene of several grisly murders.

For a small community group, the Chester Little Theatre company has had some very striking productions in its home in the Powell Theater building. The same can be said of many of its ghosts. Located on Wylie Street at the site of what had once been the town's telephone company, speculation about the presence of ghosts in the old theater building has been taking place for decades, and perhaps even longer. The area around the structure has had a long and diverse life—the city morgue, the telephone company, an old movie theater, and various other businesses have stood in this spot over the years. Various unexplained sights and sounds have taken place here as well.

Although it is not officially recorded in the city records, many of the town's older residents believe that the area around the Chester Little Theatre was used as the gallows, or public hanging grounds, back in the late 1780s. (The gallows have also been reported to be located at various other sites throughout the city, such as the old city jail, which would make much more sense.) If this area *had* been the site of the old gallows, however, perhaps the theatre's ghosts are those of the condemned who had been executed there.

A more likely story is that the theater's main ghost dates back to the 1930s, when the Chester Telephone Company occupied the space where the theater building is now. At that time, the company was owned and operated by the Bell family (who in spite of their family business were no relation to Alexander Graham Bell). The operators who handled the long-distance calls for the company were situated at 109 Wylie Street (now the offices for the Chester Associate Reformed Presbyterian Church, also said to be haunted). Next to them was Barron's Funeral Home at 105 Wylie (which could also account for some of the haunting activity there!); the funeral home still exists today, although further down the street. Finally, the City (now known as the Powell) Theater was located next door at 103 Wylie.

According to the *Chester Reporter* newspaper, on July 14, 1932, a young man by the name of Daniel Bell was preparing to take a bath in the shower provided for employees in the telephone company basement on Wylie Street. He struck a match to light the lamp there, and set alight some escaping gas, causing the main boiler to explode. Mr. Bell was severely burned in the explosion, but managed to make it upstairs to where three female telephone operators were on duty, helping them escape with only minor injuries. Mr. Bell himself died of his injuries two days later.

The most commonly told version of this story, though, is that Mr. Bell was actually preparing for his bath in the basement of Barron's Funeral Home, and the boiler explosion was blamed on a faulty pilot light. Regardless of where the accident took place or what caused it, however, Mr. Bell's bravery in saving the three phone operators is still true.

But is it his ghost that haunts the theater? In addition to Daniel Bell, as well as prospective spirits from the old gallows, the city morgue, and the funeral home, there is rumor that a woman was murdered in the alley beside the building in the 1970s. As with the gallows, however, there appears to be no factual evidence to confirm this. Town lore also states that an African-American woman was raped in the "blacks-only" balcony of the theater in the 1950s; during the struggle with her attackers, she fell or was thrown down the concrete steps, where she bumped her head and died. Several researchers who have investigated the balcony and stairs have reported cold spots, feelings of sickness, and a choking sensation as they walked through the area.

While there may be doubt as to who the theater's otherworldly residents actually may be, there is no doubt that otherworldly activity takes place in the building. Unexplained sounds, such as footsteps and voices, have been heard in the theatre by people who are supposedly there alone. One theater researcher reported that he had once heard the unmistakable sound of the slapping of film in a projector's take-up reel from upstairs, even though the theater had long since ceased to be a movie house and the old projector was no longer there. There have even been several cases of researchers catching electronic voice phenomenon (EVP)—disembodied voices or other sounds caught on an electronic recording device, although not heard at the time of the recording.

One startling instance of an EVP of sorts is the disturbing story of sounds picked up during one play rehearsal on the headsets used by the theater technicians, although the sounds were not heard anywhere else in the theatre. According to the story, the stage manager working the rehearsal stepped out from behind the curtain at one point and was clearly quite shaken. The manager had the crew come and listen to the headset she was wearing, and they all heard the unmistakable sound of a baby crying. The cries were coming in quite clearly through the headset, but the cast and crew members were the only ones in the theater, and there was no baby with them.

The most terrifying tale to come out of the Chester Little Theatre revolves around what happened with an ordinary cassette tape and player. The cast was presenting *Man of La Mancha,* and was using a tape of the play's songs to practice with during rehearsals. One of the songs in the play, which was sung by the priest, was in Latin and was known as "The Death Song." Listening to a Latin dirge could be morbid enough, but the story took an eerie and unnerving twist when the company left the recorder and tape on stage after rehearsal one night and returned to it the following day.

When they played the tape back, the cast and crew were startled to hear the Latin death song coming out of the speaker *backwards.* The rest of the songs, however, were perfectly normal. In addition to the eerie sounds, other unusual anomalies such as multiple odd lights and even apparitions in various parts of the theater have been seen. One company member spoke of seeing two cylinders of light appear on the stage, and watched as they moved back and forth with no apparent light source to account for them. Other researchers have reported seeing a series of lights on stage in the otherwise darkened theatre. There have also been at least two separate accounts of a man being seen in the balcony, and one of a woman in a long black dress in the stairway leading up to the balcony. In each of these cases, the apparition faded away.

The company of the Chester Little Theatre has since moved to a new location, and their former home stands empty—that is, except for its ghosts. Perhaps, now that they have the stage to themselves, the building's ghostly inhabitants are acting out dramas of their own.

LONGSTREET THEATRE

UNIVERSITY OF SOUTH CAROLINA AT COLUMBIA

> The ghosts of Confederate soldiers are thought to wander the basement of this former military hospital—and something much more sinister lurks in the Catacombs below.

The University of South Carolina is a state research university situated in the capital city and located not far from the South Carolina State House in downtown Columbia. Originally founded in 1801 as South Carolina College, the school attempted to promote harmony between the residents of the Backcountry and the coastal Lowcountry of the state. During the Civil War, the college became a symbol of the South as many of its students joined the Confederate Army; and in fact, the school was forced to close for several years during the war due to a sharp drop in enrollment and attendance. However, the school reopened again in 1866, and during Reconstruction was the only college in the South to admit and grant degrees to African Americans (although this victory was short-lived as the school closed once again only to re-open only to whites). In 1906, the institution was re-chartered as the University of South Carolina, and rapidly grew to become the state's most popular institution of higher learning.

Located deep in the heart of campus is the Horseshoe, the site of the school's original nineteenth-century campus. The first building constructed there as part of the college was Rutledge Chapel, which served not only as the school chapel, but also as a residence hall, administrative office, and classroom at the same time. Shortly after that, North Building (later DeSaussure College) was constructed nearby, and was originally designed for dormitory facilities in its east and west wings with academic facilities in its center portion. Eventually, additional buildings around these two were constructed in the shape of a horseshoe, with nine buildings taking shape over the following forty-plus years. The Horseshoe's buildings

Longstreet Theatre on the USC campus. Could a strange being known as the "Third-Eye-Man" roam the old tunnels beneath the building? *Photo courtesy of Jennifer DeVoll.*

have survived an earthquake, fire, and the upheaval of the Civil War and Reconstruction periods. Today, it includes residence halls, the student union, numerous academic buildings, various sports facilities, and the Longstreet Theatre.

Part of the original nineteenth-century Horseshoe, the Roman-temple Longstreet Theatre building was constructed in 1855, and was designed originally as a chapel and auditorium for the college's growing enrollment. The building encountered numerous difficulties almost from the very beginning. Construction was two years behind schedule, the roof was blown off twice, and poor acoustics in the auditorium apparently could not be improved. The building (along with others on the Horseshoe) was put into use as a military hospital during the Civil War, and the South Carolina state legislature met there briefly after the war was over. During Reconstruction, the building housed an armory and arsenal for the state inspector general, and finally (owing to the fact that the acoustical problem was never solved, making it unsuitable for a performance space), it was converted into a science facility in 1888. It later became a gymnasium in 1893.

Finally in 1976, the building was suitably remodeled for use as a theatre, and was put into service for the school's Department of Theatre & Speech. The original two-story building grew to four, and featured a circular stage surrounded by seating. Technical systems were added, and an adjacent building, formerly a swimming pool, was turned into a costume shop and stage support area. The theatre was named for Augustus B. Longstreet, a controversial writer and educator who served as president of the South Carolina college from 1857 to 1861.

With such a rich and colorful history, it's not to be wondered at that Longstreet is rumored to be haunted. Many stories have circulated among the student population of strange sights and sounds in the building, especially at night. It has long been rumored that during its time as a Civil War military hospital, the basement of Longstreet was in fact the hospital morgue, in a room that now serves as the Green Room for the theatre. The Green Room is made of three barrel-vaulted brick alcoves, and is one of the only areas in the building that has changed very little since the nineteenth century. Stories have been told of objects moving around, "cold spots," and uneasy feelings in the basement.

One well-known campus story relates an experience one student had while in the theatre late at night for a dress rehearsal. She had gone to the basement to buy a soda from the vending machine directly across from the Green Room, and was facing the machine when she felt a sudden wave of fear. Turning to look behind her, she saw nothing, but felt the temperature drop suddenly and felt a wall of cold air hit her even though there are no windows in the basement and the doors were closed. The student left immediately, and later stated that she felt she had been watched while in the basement.

Since then, students have reported other incidents such as being shoved or touched, hearing a man's voice, and a general feeling of being watched. Many believe that the ghosts of the Confederate soldiers who died at the hospital are responsible for the strange occurrences, and who for the most part, are friendly—unless, of course, you happen to be from the North. So convinced are many of the students and staff of the building's haunting that many refuse to be in the basement alone after dark, and have reportedly instituted an unofficial buddy system.

Longstreet's best-known "ghost story," however, may not be about a ghost at all. Running underneath the theater, and in fact much of the rest of the campus, are a series of heat and utility tunnels known as "The Catacombs." The very nature of the tunnels—dark, damp, and closed off for safety reasons—makes them seem especially sinister, and has given rise to multiple reports of supernatural occurrences that seem to have little basis in fact. One account, though, does have a strong sense of credibility, with a number of believable eyewitness reports providing a physical description of a strange being apparently residing in the underground tunnels.

According to school records at the university, the first reported sighting of this odd creature took place on November 12, 1949. The account states that on this date, two students walking near Longstreet Theatre spotted "a strange man dressed in bright silver" in the road.[19] Before the astonished young men could get closer, the thing opened a manhole cover and crawled inside, pulling the cover closed and disappearing into the sewers.

One of the students who witnessed the strange occurrence was Christopher Nichols, a writer for the student newspaper *The Gamecock*. Nichols composed an article about what he dubbed "the Sewer Man," and word quickly spread around campus. After a few weeks, though, the initial hype created by his article died down when no further eyewitness sightings were reported.

It didn't take long, however, for the furor to build back up again. About six months later, on April 7, 1950, a campus security officer was patrolling the area behind Longstreet when he stumbled across the remains of two mutilated chickens. Feathers and other parts of the birds were scattered all over the theater's loading dock. His first thought was that this was most likely a college prank or perhaps part of a fraternity hazing activity. Following standard procedure, he radioed a report from his patrol car, and returned to the building to investigate further.

When he arrived back at the theater building, he was startled to find what appeared to be a man dressed in silver bent over the chicken scraps. Turning his flashlight on the being, the policeman was shocked when the figure stared back at him and revealed a grotesque, oddly-colored face, with what appeared to be a third eye directly in the center of its forehead. It was small, but an eye just the same.

Shaken badly by this eerie encounter, the officer ran immediately back to his car and called for back up. After promptly responding to their colleague's summons, the other officers accompanied him to the rear of the theatre, but could find no sign of the "third-eye-man." The only evidence in sight was several chicken feathers and bones still strewn about the theater's loading area, and the fact that the first officer was clearly in a state of near-hysteria. In spite of the obvious sincerity of his emotional state, though, the officer who had encountered the strange being was unable to convince his fellow officers of what he had seen.

It was thought that perhaps this encounter would be the last of the third-eye or sewer man, but that was not the case. Almost twenty years passed before any further sightings of the creature occurred, but in October 1960, yet another report was made of an encounter with the strange being. On one night in early October, several fraternity brothers took three pledges into the Catacombs for a pledge ritual. They descended the tunnels and proceeded towards the Horseshoe. According to police reports of the incident, they had no sooner turned the first corner when they were met by "a crippled-looking man dressed all in silver."

The pledges at first assumed this was part of the ritual; but it didn't take them long to realize this was no joke when "the Silver Man" suddenly charged at them, wielding a metal pipe. One of the pledges, Matthew Tabor, was forced to the ground by the creature, and was reported to suffer "minor cuts and minor shock." The entire party promptly fled the tunnels, and notified the university police of the incident. The "third-eye-man hunt" began later that night, but although the police combed the tunnels for hours, there was no sign of the underground dweller.

Since then, the entrances to the tunnels have been sealed off to prevent further incidents. The general public as well as members of the university community are warned that the Catacombs are not to be entered, on pain of legal prosecution. However, sightings of the Silver Man/

The interior of Longstreet, a theatre-in-the-round. *Photo courtesy of Jennifer DeVoll.*

Sewer Man/Third-Eye-Man continued into the 1980s and the 1990s. While the university gives no credit to these accounts, maintenance workers even today will not venture into the tunnels unless it is absolutely necessary, and then will not go in alone.

Is "The Sewer Man" a ghost? Or could it possibly be something even more strange and frightening? Whatever he may be, just remember that if you ever find yourself at the Longstreet Theater and feel an unexplained presence, hear ghostly sounds, or see a three-eyed man dressed all in silver, there may be much more to it than theatrical effects and characters from the university's Department of Dramatic Art.

THE HAZEL B. ABBOT THEATRE (WILSON HALL)

CONVERSE COLLEGE, SPARTANBURG

> Staff and students alike are always careful to pay their respects to "Miss Hazel."

Located in the Upstate region of South Carolina, Converse College is a liberal arts women's school dedicated to higher education for and enterprise among women of all backgrounds and interests. It was founded in 1890 by Dexter Edgar Converse, a Vermont native who had settled in Spartanburg just prior to the Civil War. Converse had grown extremely successful in the cotton industry, and became interested in establishing a college for women so that his daughter, Marie, and others like her could have every possible educational advantage.

When Converse College first opened its doors in 1890, the Main Hall (as it was then called) was the only building on campus. Before the Civil War, several attempts had been made to establish various religious institutions on the site, and the main hall of St. John's Seminary had already been partially completed when the Converse Board of Directors purchased the property from the Episcopal Diocese. The hall was completed

A portrait of "Miss Hazel" hangs in the lobby of the theater that bears her name. Flowers are left under the painting at the opening of every performance out of respect for her spirit that is said to still be there. *Photo courtesy of the author.*

for the opening of the new women's school, and in the following years additional structures were added on either side to form a line of buildings that now dominates the Front Campus. While many of these early structures have been modernized, they still retain their original appearance more than 100 years after they were first constructed.

As enrollment at Converse grew, a new Back Campus was created behind the original buildings, with the oldest of these structures dating from 1912. In January 1892, a fire destroyed the Main Hall. The cornerstone for the present building was laid in April 1892 on the site of the burned structure, with the exterior being similar in design to that of the original building. During Converse's formative years, this building served as a center for many of the school's activities, as well as housing for faculty/students, classrooms, a dining hall, and administration offices. In 1929, the Main Building

The interior lobby of the Hazel B. Abbot Theatre in Wilson Hall on the Converse College Campus. *Photo courtesy of the author.*

was renamed Wilson Hall in honor of B.F. Wilson, the first president of Converse.

Wilson Hall currently houses the Gee Dining Room, a well as the admissions and administrative offices for the school. It also is home to two active theatre spaces that serve the school's Department of Theatre and Dance—the Laird Studio Theatre and The Hazel B. Abbot Theatre, a 279-seat proscenium theater where many of the department's main productions are staged.

The theater space was named for Hazel Belle Abbot, who was the Professor of Speech and Drama at Converse from 1927 to 1937. Later she served as the chairman of the department from 1937 until 1956. It is said to be her ghost haunting the space that bears her name. Regardless of what she may have been like when she worked at the school, "Miss Hazel" (as the ghost is known) is reputed to not be very friendly. Strange noises attributed to her have been heard in the Prop Room, and a cold presence is felt in the theater, especially if one is sitting in "her" seat in the auditorium! Out of respect for Miss Hazel, a seat dedicated to her is left unsold at every performance, and if one should happen to sit there, they reportedly feel extremely uncomfortable for quite some time afterwards. Flowers are also left under her portrait on the opening night of every performance, to ensure a good run.

According to Lily Knights, a former Converse student who performed in plays while at the school, "Hazel will get upset if you don't show her respect; it's her theater." She also went on to state that in spite of the efforts made by students and faculty to stay on Miss Hazel's good side, things can still go awry. "During [one production] in the spring of 2004, everybody in the crew had headphones to communicate with each other. In the middle of the play, these red lights came on and started beeping constantly. They were new headphones. The stage manager got all freaked out."[20]

The Palmetto Players company at Converse is one of the oldest college theatre groups in the state, and is open to anyone with an interest in theatre, not just department majors. Members of the group provide support both on and off the stage for Theatre/Converse, the college's undergraduate academic program. The program produces comedy, drama, and improv in seasonal offerings open to the public. Anyone is welcome to attend a performance at Converse—just so long as they don't sit in Miss Hazel's seat!

THE DOCK STREET THEATRE

CHARLESTON

> The father of presidential assassin John Wilkes Booth is thought to haunt this historic playhouse, as does the spirit of an ambitious but unfortunate courtesan.

The Dock Street Theatre, located in the heart of Charleston's downtown historic district, is said to be one of the most haunted places in the city. Originally constructed in 1736 on what was then Dock (now Queen) Street, the theater opened on January 24, 1737, with a performance of George Farquhar's *The Recruiting Officer*. Numerous plays and operas were staged at the Dock Street over the next few years, and the theater became an integral part of Charleston's social life.

In 1740, a massive fire struck the city that completely destroyed a large number of historic buildings, including the theater. Very little was done to the site until 1809, when it was purchased by Charlestonian Alexander Calder and his wife. The couple financed the construction of a hotel on the former theater site and surrounding city block, and shortly thereafter the Planter's Hotel opened its doors.

Over the next few years, the hotel was developed into a fashionable resort that attracted a wide variety of high-society and other well-known guests. One of these was Junius Brutus Booth, father of presidential assassin

The Dock Street Theatre as it undergoes renovations in 2008. *Photo courtesy of the author.*

John Wilkes Booth who was responsible for the death of Abraham Lincoln in 1865. Booth Sr. was a guest at the hotel in 1838, along with the theatrical troupe to which he belonged while they were performing in Charleston. It was said that Booth attempted to murder the troupe's manager while they were staying at the hotel—like father, like son!—but fortunately, the attempt was unsuccessful.

Another guest at the hotel was a young lady by the name of Nettie Dickerson. An ambitious but poor and naïve young woman, Nettie had come to Charleston in 1838 from her small South Carolina hometown, in the hopes of marrying a wealthy merchant or businessman. It was her dream to escape from her poor background and upbringing, and establish herself in wealthy Charleston society.

It didn't take Nettie long to realize that high-society men would not be interested in marrying a poor working-class girl, particularly one who at twenty-five years old was well past prime marrying age. However, Nettie discovered she could do very well as a paid escort, and soon became highly sought after in that capacity. She left her job at St. Philip's Episcopal Church and spent most of her evenings at the Planter's Hotel with her clients.

Although Nettie eventually became very wealthy, she was still unhappy. Her work as an escort allowed her to see the high-society lifestyle she wanted, but kept her from being able to achieve it. To escape the hopelessness of her situation, she would often stand by herself on the hotel's balcony, leaning against the wrought-iron railing and taking in the beautiful view of the city below. Many times she would stay out even when storms threatened and swept through the city, enjoying the feel of the rain and the display of lightning and thunder.

One ill-fated evening, as Nettie was standing in her favorite spot on the balcony, a thunder storm approached and drew dangerously close. She remained where she was to enjoy the rain as she had often done before, but this night the very storm that brought her so much joy also brought about her destruction. As Nettie leaned against the balcony, a bolt of lightning struck the metal railing near where she was standing, killing her instantly.

Eventually, the Planter's Hotel slowly began to fall into disuse and disrepair, and by the 1930s, it was in ruins. In 1935, the City of Charleston purchased the site with funds from President Roosevelt's Works Progress Administration. The city decided to restore the building to its original purpose as a theater, although not necessarily as an exact reconstruction of the first theater building. According to federal architect Douglas Ellington, the new theater was being built in modern fashion, with up-to-date equipment, but would "carry the same spirit" as the original. Local architect Alfred Simmons used native wood along with railings, windows, mantels, and other refurbished items that had been salvaged from area buildings to maintain the historical feel.[21]

Once the renovation had been completed, the Dock Street Theatre re-opened on November 26, 1937, with a grand gala event and a modified version of *The Recruiting Officer*, the original opening play. The theater and its resident acting company, the Footlight Players, have continued to offer numerous productions and events ever since. In particular, the theater serves as the site of many of the activities that make up Spoleto, Charleston's premier arts festival held every spring; and, as before in its early days, the theater is an integral part of the city's social life.

The ghosts of both Nettie Dickerson and Junius Brutus Booth are believed to haunt the Dock Street Theatre. (One Charleston tour guide mentioned to me that it was rumored the ghost of a Confederate soldier had been seen in the building as well, but there seemed to be no other stories or evidence to support this.) Local theater-goers and visitors to the city alike have reported catching fleeting glimpses of Nettie standing in her favorite spot on the balcony, wearing a long red dress. She has also been seen in the second floor hallway. In addition, strange noises (such as the sound of someone out of breath), lights that turn themselves on and off, and moving objects have been reported that have been attributed to Junius Booth. His spirit has never been seen, but his presence is apparently often felt.

The Dock Street Theatre is scheduled to re-open in 2010 after renovations. It will be interesting to see if the construction work will have disturbed Booth and Nettie, and stir up any further "ghostly" activity in the theater. According to one of the construction foremen I spoke with, he himself had not experienced anything out of the ordinary during the construction process, but that one of his men had reported several odd occurrences (although apparently this particular worker had often done that before!). The foreman did tell me, however, that one "ghost hunting" group conducting research in the theater reported a wide variety of unusual sights and sounds, and that they felt the building was indeed extremely haunted.

If you ever find yourself visiting the city of Charleston, be sure to stop by the Dock Street Theatre, and perhaps even take in a show. In addition to its reputation as the most haunted building in the city, the theater is on the National Historic Landmark registry, and definitely captures the feel of old historic Charleston. You may find not only the spirit of the city, but the spirits of Booth and Nettie as well.

AFTERWARD

During the course of my research for this project, I was pleasantly surprised to discover just how many haunted theaters were in my own backyard—my home state of North Carolina and its neighboring state of South Carolina—and to learn the captivating histories and stories behind each one. I was equally surprised to learn of the number of other theaters that supposedly had their own ghost legends and lore, but that I was unable to find any solid information on in time for the printing of this book. These include the Owen Theater at Mars Hill College near Asheville, North Carolina; the Turnage Theater in Washington, North Carolina; Greenville Little Theater in Greenville, South Carolina; the Newberry Opera House in Newberry, South Carolina; and the former (and now-demolished) home of the Charlotte Children's Theater in Charlotte, North Carolina (although it is my goal to chronicle that story in a future work!).

My intent through the course of this work was to make certain I had credible corroborating stories and evidence for each ghost story before I committed these stories to print. So my apologies if I have missed a thrilling tale from any of these theaters—I hope to be able to still add them to my own collection in the near future.

END NOTES

[1]Alan Brown, *Shadows and Cypress*, Jackson, Mississippi (University Press of Mississippi, 2004), 98-99.

[2]Daniel Barefoot, *Haunted Halls of Ivy Ghosts of Southern Colleges and Universities*, Winston-Salem, North Carolina (John F. Blair, 2004), 116.

[3]"'Ghoulies and Ghosties' Stories Fly At Carolina About Things That Go 'Bump in the Night,'" *University Gazette On-line* 19 Oct 05.

[4]Landry Haarman and Caryn Washington, "The Ghosts of Dana Auditorium," *The Guilfordian* 3 Nov 06.

[5]Landry Haarman and Caryn Washington, "The Ghosts of Dana Auditorium," *The Guilfordian* 3 Nov 06.

[6]Taylor Shain, "The Ghosts Around Us," *GoTriad.com* 26 Oct 06.

[7]"Stage Fright," UNC-G Alumni & Friends newsletter 6 Oct 08.

[8]"A Brief History of the Carolina Theatre," 5 Aug O8 (http//www.carolinatheatre.com/History.html).

[9]"The Old Courthouse Theatre," *ScaredyPantsNC.com* 10 Aug 08 (http//scaredypantsnc.blogspot.com/2007/10/old-courthouse-theatre.html).

[10]Michael Johnstone, "The History of the Carolina Theatre" 12 Sep 08 (http//www.theatreorgans.com/nc/metrolina/carolina/historyoftheatre.html).

[11]Michael Johnstone, "The History of the Carolina Theatre." 12 Sep 08 (http//www.theatreorgans.com/nc/metrolina/carolina/historyoftheatre.html).

[12]Stephanie Burt Williams, *Ghost Stories of Charlotte & Mecklenburg County Remnants of the Past in a New South* (Winston-Salem, North Carolina Bandit Press, 2003), 57.

[13]Stephanie Burt Williams, *Ghost Stories of Charlotte & Mecklenburg County Remnants of the Past in a New South* (Winston-Salem, North Carolina Bandit Press, 2003), 57.

[14]Stephanie Burt Williams, *Ghost Stories of Charlotte & Mecklenburg County Remnants of the Past in a New South* (Winston-Salem, North Carolina Bandit Press, 2003), 58.

[15]Michael Johnstone, "The History of the Carolina Theatre." 12 Sep 08 (http//www.theatreorgans.com/nc/metrolina/carolina/historyoftheatre. html).

[16]Stephanie Burt Williams, *Ghost Stories of Charlotte & Mecklenburg County Remnants of the Past in a New South* (Winston-Salem, North Carolina Bandit Press, 2003), 20.

[17]Stephanie Burt Williams, *Ghost Stories of Charlotte & Mecklenburg County Remnants of the Past in a New South* (Winston-Salem, North Carolina Bandit Press, 2003), 19.

[18]Jennifer Jones, "Abbeville Opera House Known for 'Ghost Chair,'" *Anderson Independent-Mail* 23 Oct 05.

[19]Daniel Barefoot, *Haunted Halls of Ivy Ghosts of Southern Colleges and Universities* (Winston-Salem, North Carolina John F. Blair, 2004), 27.

[20]"HauntedConverseCollege," *askyewolf.com* 12 Nov 07 (http//www.askyewolfe. com/HauntedConverseCollege.html).

[21]Robert P. Stockton, "Former Planter's Hotel Wins National Acclaim." *The News and Courier* 16 Jul 73 1-B.

BIBLIOGRAPHY

askyewolf.com. "HauntedConverseCollege." 12 Nov 07 (http//www.askyewolfe.com/HauntedConverseCollege.html).

Barefoot, Daniel W. *Piedmont Phantoms*. Winston-Salem, North Carolina John F. Blair, 2002.

Barefoot, Daniel W. *Haunted Halls of Ivy Ghosts of Southern Colleges and Universities*. Winston-Salem, North Carolina. John F. Blair, 2004.

"A Brief History of the Carolina Theatre." Carolina Theater, 5 Aug 08. (http//www.carolinatheatre.com/History.html).

Brown, Alan. *Shadows and Cypress*. Jackson, Mississippi. University Press of Mississippi, 2004.

"'Ghoulies and Ghosties' Stories Fly At Carolina About Things That Go 'Bump in the Night.'" *University Gazette On-line*, 19 Oct 05.

Haarman, Landry and Caryn Washington. "The Ghosts of Dana Auditorium." *The Guilfordian*, 3 Nov 06.

Johnson, Talmadge. *Ghosts of the South Carolina Upcountry*. Charleston, South Carolina. The History Press, 2005.

Johnstone, Michael. "The History of the Carolina Theatre." 12 Sep 08. (http//www.theatreorgans.com/nc/metrolina/carolina/historyoftheatre.html).

Jones, Jennifer. "Abbeville Opera House Known for 'Ghost Chair.'" *Anderson Independent-Mail*, 23 Oct 05.

Nickens, Eddie. "Going Upcountry." *Historic Preservation* Mar/Apr 2002. 18-20.

"Opera House Project Revitalized Abbeville." *Saluda Standard Sentinel*, 21 Jan 88.

Roberts, Nancy. *Ghosts from the Coasts: A Ghostly Tour of Coastal North Carolina, South Carolina, and Georgia.* Chapel Hill, North Carolina. The University of North Carolina Press, 2001.

ScaredyPantsNC.com, "The Old Courthouse Theatre."10 Aug 08. (http//scaredypantsnc.blogspot.com/2007/10/old-courthouse-theatre.html).

Shain, Taylor. "The Ghosts Around Us." *GoTriad.com,* 26 Oct 06.

"Stage Fright." UNC-G Alumni & Friends newsletter, 6 Oct 08.

Stockton, Robert P. "Former Planter's Hotel Wins National Acclaim." *The News and Courier,* 16 Jul 73 1-B.

Stockton, Robert P. "Theater Recreates Old Splendor." *The News and Courier,* 25 May 81 1-B.

Rivenbark, Tony. *Thalian Hall A Brief History.* Wilmington, North Carolina. Thalian Hall, 2008.

"The Old Courthouse Theatre." *ScaredyPantsNC.com.* 10 Aug 08. http//scaredypantsnc.blogspot.com/2007/10/old-courthouse-theatre.html.

Williams, Stephanie Burt. *Ghost Stories of Charlotte & Mecklenburg County Remnants of the Past in a New South.* Winston-Salem. North Carolina Bandit Press, 2003.

Zepke, Terrance. *The Best Ghost Tales of North Carolina.* Sarasota, Florida. Pineapple Press, 2001.

Zepke, Terrance. *The Best Ghost Tales of South Carolina.* Sarasota, Florida. Pineapple Press, 2004.

Zepke, Terrance. *Ghosts of the Carolina Coast Haunted Lighthouses, Plantations, and Other Historic Sites.* Sarasota, Florida. Pineapple Press, 1999.

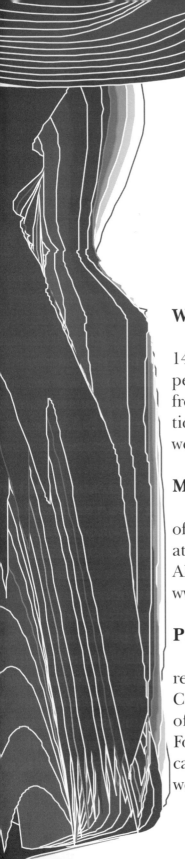

HAUNTED THEATERS CONTACT INFORMATION

Waterside Theatre

The Waterside Theatre is located at 1409 National Park Drive in Manteo, and performances of *The Lost Colony* run nightly from May-August. For information, call the ticket office at 252-473-3414, or visit the website at www.thelostcolony.org/.

Messick Theatre Arts Center

For information on public performances offered at the Messick Theatre Arts Center at ECU, call 252-328-6829 or 1-800-ECU-ARTS (1-800-328-2787), or visit online at www.ecuarts.com.

Playmakers Repertory Company

Playmakers Repertory Company performs regularly at the Paul Green Theater in the Center for Dramatic Art on the University of North Carolina-Chapel Hill campus. For performance and ticket information, call 919-962-PLAY, or visit the Playmaker's website at www.playmakersrep.org/.

Memorial Hall

Memorial Hall is located on East Cameron Avenue on the University of North Carolina-Chapel Hill campus, and offers a wide variety of artistic and educational performances. For information, call the ticket office at 919-843-3333, or visit on-line at www.carolinaperformingarts.org/.

Dana Auditorium

Dana Auditorium is on the Guilford College campus at 5800 West Friendly Avenue in Greensboro. To learn more about public offerings and/or to purchase tickets, visit the website at www.guilford.edu/yeararts.

Carolina Theatre

The Carolina Theatre is at 310 South Greene Street, Greensboro, North Carolina 27410. For show and ticket information, call the box office at 336-333-2605, or visit the website at www.carolinatheatre.com.

Old Court House Theatre Company

The Old Court House Theatre Company can be found in their current home at 49 Spring Street NW in Concord. For performance and ticket information, call the office at 704-788-2405, or visit the website at www.oldcourthousetheatre.org.

Thalian Hall

Thalian Hall is located at 310 Chestnut Street in historic downtown Wilmington. For performance and ticket information, contact the box office at 910-343-3664 (toll free 800-523-2820), or visit on-line at http://www.thalianhall.org/.

Carolina Theatre

The Carolina Theatre is located in the heart of downtown Charlotte, and occasionally hosts artistic performances and other cultural activities. For more information on the theater restoration project or upcoming events, visit the website at http://www.carolinatheatre.us.

Spirit Square

Spirit Square is part of the North Carolina Blumenthal Performing Arts Center, located on North College Street in downtown Charlotte. For ticket information, contact the box office at 704-372-1000, or visit on-line at www.blumenthalcenter.org/.

ImaginOn

ImaginOn offers a wide variety of performances, exhibits, and other artistic activities, and is

located at 300 East Seventh Street in
Charlotte. For more information, call
the main office at 704-973-2780, or go
on-line at www.imaginon.org/.

Theatre Charlotte

Theatre Charlotte is located at 501
Queens Road in Charlotte. For show
and ticket information, call the box
office 704-376-3777, or visit on-line at
www.theatrecharlotte.org.

Regal Manor Theatre

The Regal Manor Theatre offers
a wide variety of film genres, and
is found at 607 Providence Road in
Charlotte. For ticket information,
call the box office at 704-334-2727.

Carolina Theater

The Carolina Theater in Hickory
is located at 222 1st Avenue NW. For
show times and ticket information,
call the box office at 828-322-
7210, or visit the website at www.
carolinatheater-hickory.com.

Abbeville Opera House

The Abbeville Opera House is
at 100 Court Square in Abbeville.
To learn more about season
performances and for ticket
information, contact the box office

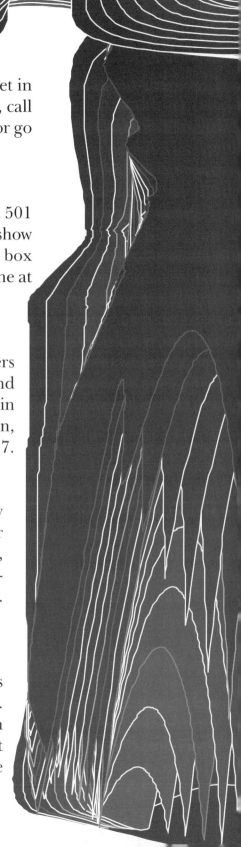

at 864-366-2157, or go on-line at http://www. theabbevilleoperahouse. com/.

Chester Little Theatre Company

While the Chester Little Theatre Company no longer performs in the Powell Theater building, the company continues to offer a variety of dramatic performances to the community. They are currently located at 100 Cesterian Square in Chester. For show and ticket information, call the office at 803-377-1101, e-mail chesterlittletheatre@ yahoo.com, or visit the website at http://www. chesterlittletheatre.com.

Longstreet Theatre

Longstreet Theatre is located at the intersection of Green and Sumter Streets on the University of South Carolina campus in Columbia. For performance and ticket information, contact the office by phone at 803-777-4288, by email at theatre@sc.edu, or visit the Department of Theatre and Dance website at www.cas.sc.edu/thea/.

Hazel B. Abbot Theatre

The Hazel B. Abbot Theatre is in Wilson Hall on the Converse College campus. For information on public offerings, call the office at 864-596-9068, or visit on-line at http://www.converse.edu/academics/majors/theatreevents.asp.

Dock Street Theatre

The Dock Street Theatre is located at 135 Church Street in Charleston. As of this writing, it is currently undergoing renovation, but is scheduled to reopen in the summer of 2009. For information on the opening and upcoming performances, call 843-720-3968, or visit the website at www.charlestonstage.com.

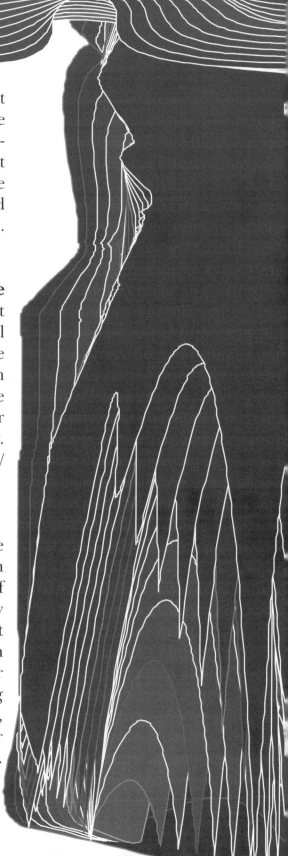

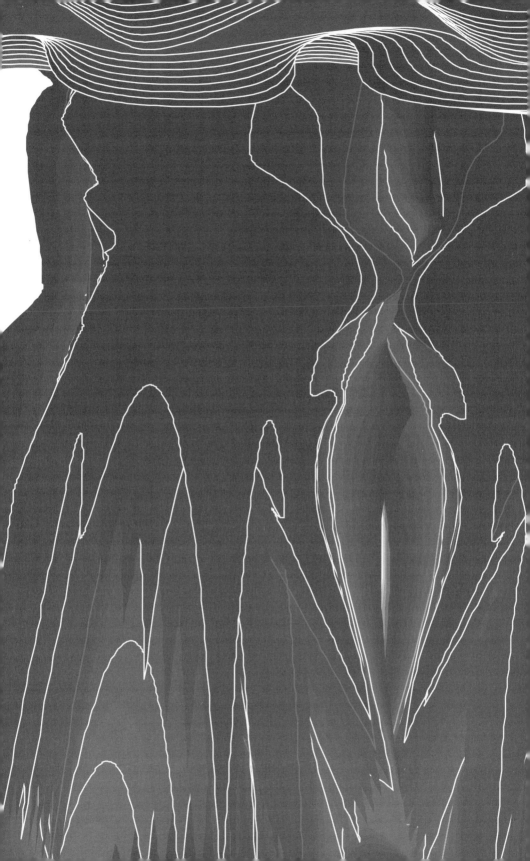

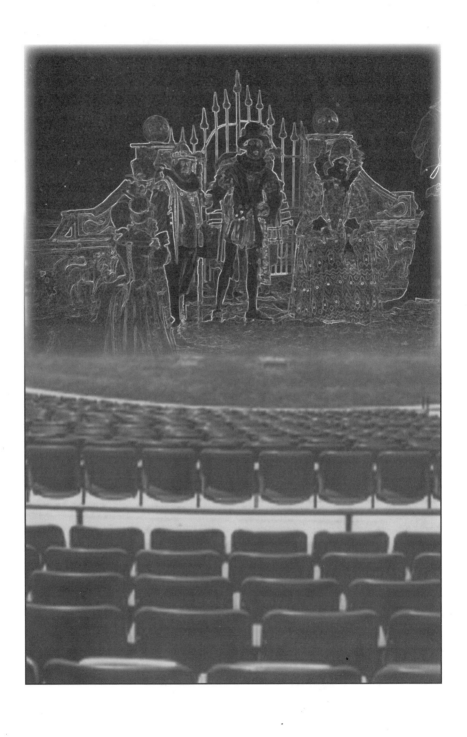